DATE DUE

MR 1 5 '79		
		PRINTED IN U.S.A.

DATE DUE

		PRINTED IN U.S.A.

Woodin, G. Bruce
    Revolution and constitution 1763-1797; vol. 2.
N.Y., Sterling, [1970]
    96p.   illus.,maps (A fresh look at
American history)

    1.Constitution-U.S.   2.U.S.-History-Revolution.
I.Title.   II.Series.

REVOLUTION
and CONSTITUTION
(1763 - 1797)

G. BRUCE WOODIN

A Fresh Look At
AMERICAN HISTORY
Volume 2

 STERLING PUBLISHING CO., INC.   NEW YORK

ACKNOWLEDGMENTS

The Author and Publisher wish to thank the following people for their advice and suggestions in regard to this volume and for having oriented the material to the social studies curriculum in the elementary schools, as well as for checking the terminology for easy reading in intermediate grades, beginning at fourth grade level:

Elizabeth Noon
Editor, *The Instructor*

Ada A. Towne
Curriculum Coordinator (Social Studies)
Elementary Schools
Board of Education, City of New York

Lucille Harris
Corrective Reading Teacher
P.S. 132, The Bronx, New York

The Author and the Publisher also wish to thank the staff of the Schomburg Collection of Negro Literature and History of the New York Public Library for their assistance in obtaining information and pictures for this volume.

Tom Jefferson preparing his notes before writing the Declaration of Independence.

Contents

1. Problems in America 5

2. The British Move In 13

3. The Road to Revolution 21

4. The Declaration of Independence 29

5. America under Arms 39

6. The War in the North 47

7. The French Alliance 57

8. Postwar Problems and Development 69

9. A New Kind of Government 78

10. The Young Republic 86

Index 95

Crispus Attucks as he was killed by British soldiers in the "Boston Massacre." A leading patriot, he was the first black man to die for American rights.

Chapter 1

Problems in America

It was 1763. Samuel Adams, now 41 years old, felt that he was a total failure. He had never had a chance to use his excellent Harvard college education. His wife had died. The business in Boston that his father had left him was gone. The house that he had loved since he was a boy was falling apart. It was the lowest point of his life.

Now, he was a tax collector, and he hated his job—he hated to ask people for money. But he had to do it, because King George III had asked the American colonies to pay new taxes, and Sam Adams needed the job as much as Great Britain needed money.

Sam was a short, stout man who smoked a clay pipe. He spoke well, but he was handicapped by an illness called palsy, so that his voice trembled. His greatest weapon was his pen, as many people of Massachusetts knew from reading his articles in local newspapers.

Sam's pen fairly flew over the paper when King George III and

Sam Adams, a rebel by nature, used a pen rather than a gun to fight the British.

Parliament passed the Sugar Act of 1764. This new law put a high customs duty, or tax, on sugar, molasses, and other products brought into America from foreign countries. Also, it stopped the colonies from making their own coins and paper money. Besides this, British officials were given the

5

right to enter any building at any time to search for goods which had been smuggled or sneaked into the colonies without paying the customs duty.

"If we have to pay taxes without our having representation where tax laws are passed," Adams wrote, "are we not lowered from the level of British subjects to the miserable level of slaves?"

Later on, this same idea would become the battle cry of other American patriots: "No taxation without representation."

Adams could not hold his job as tax collector because of the way he felt. As far as he was concerned, the House of Commons in London, the lower house of Parliament, represented only the people of England. The American colonies had no delegates or representatives at all in Parliament, where tax laws were passed.

Sam was hoping he could get another job when the merchants in Massachusetts decided to join in a "non-importation agreement" —that is, they agreed not to import, or bring in, goods from Great Britain. Sam, pen in hand, wrote a letter which he sent to the other colonies, suggesting that they join together to oppose the Sugar Act.

While this "fire" burned, another started. General Thomas Gage, commander of all British soldiers in America, wanted the colonists to furnish housing and

One of the stamps required under the Stamp Act for the taxing of papers and documents.

food for his men free of charge. So he got Parliament to pass the so-called Quartering Act.

To top this off, another law, the Stamp Act of 1765, placed a heavy tax on every colonist, rich or poor. Almost all papers and documents—including school diplomas, marriage licenses and newspapers—were to carry a tax stamp sold by the British Government. As Adams saw it, the colonists were being made victims as if they were not Englishmen.

This time, Virginia led the protest, as Patrick Henry, a hot-tempered lawyer, presented to the House of Burgesses his famous "Virginia Resolutions." Using strong words, Henry reminded the House that many tyrants in the past, including Julius Caesar, had been killed for their crimes.

"And King George III may profit from their example," shouted Patrick Henry, as some of the burgesses who did not agree with him yelled "Treason!"

One night, shortly after Patrick Henry's speech, a secret meeting was held in Boston. On that night, a society was started to defend the rights of the colonists against the British King. Sam Adams became one of its leaders.

"What shall we call ourselves?" someone asked.

Someone else—it could have been Adams—replied, "The Sons of Liberty." Everyone cheered. And that was how the Sons of Liberty got its name.

The Sons of Liberty quickly went into action. Merchants stopped ordering British goods. Riots and threats of riots forced many of the British government's stamp sellers to give up their jobs. In Boston, the stamp seller was knocked about while his shop was pulled down. The rioters then turned their attention to Chief Justice Hutchinson and the customs inspectors and looted their homes.

In Charleston, South Carolina, a British official was dragged out of bed at midnight while the local Sons of Liberty searched his home for tax stamps, which they found and burned.

At a meeting held in September, 1765, Sam Adams was elected to the Massachusetts Assembly. It was a job that would take a lot of time and pay nothing. But it was just what Sam wanted. Now, as a member of the group that was supposed to make the colony's laws and

James Otis was a lawyer friend of Sam Adams and worked with him against the British in the Massachusetts Assembly.

represent the people, he could talk and write more.

Adams began to work closely with his friend James Otis, a lawyer who, as one of the four Boston representatives in the Assembly, was very powerful. Otis, at the time, was considered the leader of the Whig, or Patriot, Party.

Otis saw to it that Adams was appointed to all the important committees of the Assembly. In writing reports to the British government, whatever Otis himself wrote he gave to Adams to read and correct. It was not long before the two were the most powerful members of the Assembly.

In October, 1765, Otis and others from Massachusetts went to New York City, where delegates from nine of the American colonies were to meet. This became known as the Stamp Act Congress. The delegates wrote letters to King George III and to members of Parliament, asking them to repeal the Stamp Act. It was too late.

When November 1, 1765, dawned, almost all business in the colonies stopped. But not for long. In open defiance of the law, colonial business, without stamps, began again a few days later.

Meanwhile, trade with England froze. Non-importation went on and smuggling increased. By the end of 1765, the sale of British goods had dropped to an all-time low. Loud was the cry in England. British companies, without business, closed down. British workers, without jobs, faced starvation.

As Sam Adams said: "Nothing stings more deeply than the loss of money." In 1766, after two months of heated arguments in Parliament, the Stamp Act was repealed.

With the end of the unpopular Stamp Act, there came a deep feeling of loyalty toward England. The New York Assembly voted to put up a statue honoring King George III. In Boston, the colonists celebrated by ringing bells and firing a cannon.

More trouble with England was not long in coming and Sam Adams knew it. In 1767, after having tried many ways to raise money, Parliament passed the Townshend Acts.

These new laws put high customs duties on articles of everyday use in America—tea, glass, lead, paint, and paper. In addition, the Acts took away the right of colonial assemblies to vote their own taxes. The New York Assembly, which had refused to supply housing and food for British soldiers, was dismissed.

In coffeehouses and inns throughout the colonies, James Otis, Sam Adams, Patrick Henry, and other patriots met to talk about the Townshend Acts.

"Should we let Parliament punish a colonial assembly?" the patriots asked. "Which of our rights will they try to take away next? What other unfair taxes will they force upon us without our consent? We have no choice but to resist the new laws."

In Boston, Sam Adams drew up a strongly worded document condemning the Acts, and the Massachusetts Assembly approved it. The King's secretary for the colonies ordered members of the Assembly to withdraw the circular. He also told the British Governor to dismiss them if they did not. The Assembly refused by a vote of 92 to 17. The Governor was afraid of what the Sons of Liberty might do. So he asked for and got the army to protect him. British troops arrived from Canada to police Boston.

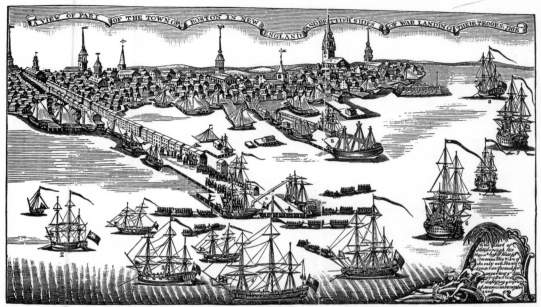

British troops arrived from Canada to police Boston upon the orders of the British governor of Massachusetts.

The feelings of the colonists were perhaps best stated in the resolutions prepared by George Washington for the Virginia House of Burgesses. These said quite clearly that only colonial assemblies had the right to force taxes on the colonists. They also did much to spread the idea of non-importation. Great Britain's trade with America was almost entirely shut off.

British merchants, losing business, asked the government to repeal the Townshend Acts. Now, King George III and Parliament seemed to realize that they had gone too far. Finally, in the spring of 1770, Parliament repealed all the customs duties except the one on tea. Hard feelings between the colonies and the mother country relaxed.

Sam Adams, James Otis, and other patriots wanted to continue non-importation until Parliament repealed the tax on tea, too. Colonial merchants, badly in need of British goods, refused to do this. Some colonial and British leaders did everything they could to maintain peace. But, in spite of their efforts, the incident they feared took place. The newspapers called it the "Boston Massacre."

The trouble began when about 20 British soldiers—who were being shouted at and stoned by Boston rioters—lost their heads and fired into the crowd. When the shooting ended, five people lay dead. One of them was a sailor named Crispus Attucks. A leading patriot, he was the first black man to die for the colonial cause.

9

As a protest against the importing of British tea, patriots, dressed up as Indians, boarded ships and dumped 342 large cases of tea into Boston Harbor. This was called the "Boston Tea Party."

John Adams, a cousin of Sam Adams and one of Boston's leading lawyers, defended the British soldiers in court. Only two of them were punished for the shooting. But the Governor, in reply to Adams's demand, withdrew British troops from Boston. The colonists relaxed, but not for long.

The British East India Company, which had been losing money on the sale of tea, asked the government for help. So the King gave the company the sole right to import tea into the American colonies. The citizens' reaction was to hold the "Boston Tea Party." On a dark night in December, 1773, about 100 patriots, dressed up as Indians, crept onto three ships that had just arrived from England. They dumped 342 large cases of precious tea into the harbor while hundreds of Bostonians watched from the docks. Someone—possibly Sam Adams—shouted, "Boston Harbor is a teapot this night!"

Things to Remember about Chapter 1

Meanings of Words and Phrases

Rebel: A person who fights authority or control, or rises in arms against his government.

Patriot: A person who loves, supports and defends his country.

Currency: Coins or paper money.

Customs duty: A tax.

Smuggle: To import or export goods secretly and illegally, without paying customs duties.

Meanings of Words and Phrases

Assembly: A legislative (law-making) group, either elected or appointed.

Representation: Having a delegate or representative in a legislature to talk for the people.

House of Burgesses: The legislature of the colony of Virginia. The word "burgesses" means "citizens."

House of Commons: The lower house of British Parliament to which members are elected by the people.

Non-importation: Refusal to import or buy imported goods.

Resolution: A written statement expressing the feelings or decisions of a group of people.

Tyrant: A harsh and unfair ruler.

Treason: In general, the attempt of a person to overthrow an existing government.

Whig: The name of a political party in Great Britain that was against taxing the colonies. For this reason, American patriots were often called Whigs.

Repeal: To do away with a law or tax.

Massacre: The killing of large numbers of people at one time.

Check Your Memory

1. What three purposes did the Sugar Act have that annoyed the colonists? (See pages 5-6.)

2. What was meant by the patriots when they said, "No taxation without representation"? (See page 6.)

3. How did it happen that the Stamp Act was never enforced? (See pages 7-8.)

4. Why did New York in particular object to the Townshend Acts? (See page 8.)

5. What would you have worn if you had been invited to the Boston Tea Party? (See page 10.)

Projects

1. Using your notebook, list the accomplishments of Samuel Adams between 1763 and 1773.

2. Pretend you were a member of the Sons of Liberty. Then send a secret message to one of your friends.

3. Get a group of your classmates to play the parts of Samuel Adams, Patrick Henry, James Otis, George Washington, and Crispus Attucks, and have them act out their feelings.

Questions for Your Classroom Discussions

1. Some people say that the wisest of men could not have settled the differences between Great Britain and the American colonies in the 1760's. Do you agree? Defend your point of view.

2. What changes would be brought about by a country's refusing to buy imported goods?

3. If you had lived in the American colonies in the 1760's, how would you have felt about paying taxes to Great Britain? Explain your answer.

REVOLUTIONARY TEA

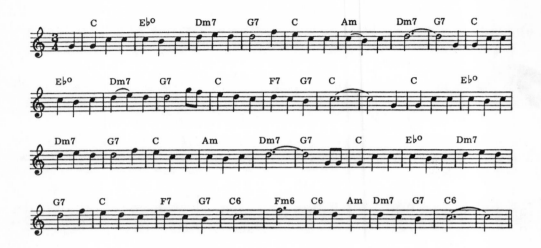

There was an old lady lived over the sea,
And she was an island queen;
Her daughter lived off in a new countrie,
With an ocean of water between.
The old lady's pockets were filled with gold,
But never contented was she,
So she called on her daughter to pay her a tax,
Of three pence a pound on the tea,
Of three pence a pound on the tea.

"Now mother, dear mother," the daughter
  replied,
"I shan't do the thing you ax;
I'm willing to pay a fair price for the tea,
But never the three penny tax."
"You shall," quoth the mother, and reddened
  with rage,
"For you're my own daughter, you see,
And sure 'tis quite proper the daughter
  should pay,
Her mother a tax on the tea,
Her mother a tax on the tea."

And so the old lady her servant called up,
And packed off a budget of tea,
And eager for three pence a pound, she put in
Enough for a large familie.
She ordered her servant to bring home the tax,
Declaring her child should obey,
Or old as she was and a woman most grown,
She'd half whip her life away,
She'd half whip her life away.

The tea was conveyed to the daughter's door,
And all down by the ocean side,
And the bouncing girl poured out every pound,
In the dark and boiling tide,
And then she called out to the island queen,
"O mother, dear mother," quoth she,
"Your tea you may have when 'tis steeped
  enough,
But never a tax from me,
But never a tax from me."

From "Songs That Changed The World," reprinted with permission of Crown Publishers, Inc.

The spirit of the Boston Tea Party was kept alive with a song called "Revolutionary Tea." It became a favorite of the patriots because it summed up America's feelings toward Britain's unfair tax on tea. Its verses had a swinging tune and called many a person's attention to the battle cry of the patriots—"No taxation without representation."

Chapter 2

The British Move In

The British, angered by the Boston Tea Party, passed a series of new laws in 1774, which the colonists called the Intolerable Acts.

The first Intolerable Act took away the charter of Massachusetts and placed the colony under the control of the British army.

The second Intolerable Act permitted British soldiers charged with crimes in America to have their cases tried in England.

The third Intolerable Act forced the people of Massachusetts to provide housing for the British soldiers who had been rushed to Boston to make the people obey the new laws.

The fourth Intolerable, or Quebec, Act extended Canada's boundaries as far south as the Ohio River and as far west as the Mississippi River. So Massachusetts, Connecticut and Virginia lost all of the lands west of the Allegheny Mountains which they believed belonged to them.

The fifth Intolerable, or Boston Port, Act caused more anger than any of the other Acts. The Port of Boston was to be closed to all shipping until the British East India Company had been paid for the tea it lost in the Boston Tea Party.

It soon became clear that Great Britain was serious about carrying out these Intolerable Acts. The colonists had fought the British government with physical force. So the British would enforce the Acts with physical force. General Thomas Gage was made Governor of Massachusetts and given extra troops to help keep order.

"The New England governments are in a state of rebellion," King George III declared. "Blows must decide whether they are to be subject to this country or independent."

Much to the surprise of the King and Parliament, the news of Boston's punishment united the colonists as never before. Supplies and help came to Boston from almost all of the colonies. Connecticut and the

It was here, in the Virginia House of Burgesses, in 1774, that Patrick Henry presented his resolution condemning the British occupation of Boston as a "hostile invasion."

Colonial Williamsburg

rest of New England sent cattle; Virginia sent 8,600 bushels of corn; the Carolinas sent rice and money; Delaware sent money; and Canada sent a thousand bushels of wheat.

Quickly, colonial assemblies gathered and discussed Boston's problem. The arguments at the meetings were heated. Men who were usually cool and calm became excited. Addressing the Virginia House of Burgesses, George Washington announced: "I'll raise a thousand men . . . and march myself at their head for the relief of Boston."

A resolution, drawn up by Patrick Henry and others, called the military occupation of Boston a "hostile invasion." The day the Boston port closed—June 1, 1774—was observed as "a day of fasting, humiliation, and prayer."

The British Governor of Virginia quickly dismissed the House of Burgesses. But before returning to their homes, the members met at the Raleigh Tavern in Williamsburg. One of them spoke for all when he said: "An attack made on one of our sister colonies . . . is an attack on all British America." A letter was then sent to the other colonies, suggesting that a meeting be held to talk about the Intolerable Acts.

The suggestion was very well received. Known as the First Continental Congress, this meeting was held in Philadelphia on September 5, 1774. Some 50 delegates met, and many of them were still deeply loyal to King George III. They still hoped that the differences between Great Britain and the colonies could be worked out peacefully. Others,

Often, the Virginia Burgesses would meet at the Raleigh Tavern in Williamsburg where they could discuss their plans in secret behind closed doors.

such as Sam Adams, felt that the time had come for Americans to fight for their rights.

The First Continental Congress did three important things. First, it drew up a Declaration of Rights, which set forth the British rights of the American colonists, including self-government. They admitted that the King had the right to disapprove laws passed by colonial assemblies, and Parliament had the right to control trade in the empire. But neither the King nor Parliament had the right to pass laws which were mainly intended to make Americans pay taxes without representation.

The second important action taken by the Congress was the formation of the Continental Association. Members were not to import or use British goods, nor were they to export goods to Britain. In each town, the Sons of Liberty would see to it that members obeyed the rules.

The third action was to ask the delegates to meet again on May 10, 1775, if the British government had not by then cancelled the Intolerable Acts.

In those days, it took weeks for sailing ships to carry mail across the Atlantic Ocean. This slowness gave the colonists the time they needed for planning before the British could make a move. The Massachusetts Assembly met in secret and organized what was called a Provincial Congress. Their first act was to name a Committee of Safety, and to lead them, John Hancock was chosen. Hancock

John Hancock used his wealth to help the citizens' army collect weapons to fight the wealthy British.

guns (cannon) from British forts and stored them at Concord.

In the same way, the Rhode Island Committee of Safety took all the ammunition from the British Fort Island post. At New Castle, New Hampshire, raiders forced British troops to hand over fighting equipment and supplies.

By the end of 1774, militia companies throughout New England were drilling. Connecticut, Rhode Island, and New Hampshire listened carefully to Hancock when he asked that they share in organizing an army. General Gage accused the Massachusetts Provincial Congress of treason, but nobody paid any attention to him.

In London, King George III

was a wealthy Boston merchant who had the interest of the people at heart. He had given a great deal of money to the Sons of Liberty and was angry at the British, who had wanted to take away his fortune. Hancock's committee was given the power to call up a citizens' army, or militia. Each militia company was to enlist one-fourth of its men "to act on a minute's notice." (That was why they were called the "Minutemen.") Artemas Ward, a veteran of the French and Indian War, was made commanding general of the Massachusetts troops.

Members of Hancock's committee were told to collect arms (weapons) wherever they could. So they stole rifles and larger

A Massachusetts patriot wearing the uniform of the hard-fighting Minutemen, who got their name because they could "act on a minute's notice."

16

was filled with rage when he found out that some Englishmen still favored the colonists as 1775 began—the year of decision set by the Continental Congress. Edmund Burke, a member of Parliament who was on the side of the Americans, called upon the British government to repeal its unjust laws and make peace. He reminded his listeners that the colonists were British subjects. These people, he said, shared the love of all Englishmen for liberty.

Delivering a brilliant speech, Burke went on to say: "Slavery they can have anywhere. It is a weed that grows in every soil. They may have it from Spain; they may have it from Prussia. But . . . freedom they can have from none but you. Deny them freedom, and you break that sole bond which originally made, and must still preserve, the unity of the empire."

By a vote of 270 to 78, Parliament refused his plea to repeal the unfair acts.

Meanwhile, the Second Massachusetts Provincial Congress took steps to get the colony ready for war. Two more generals—John Thomas and William Heath—were appointed under General Artemas Ward. A military code, the Articles of War, was adopted. The Stockbridge Indians agreed to fight with Massachusetts troops. Chosen delegates held meetings with the other New England colonies.

Edmund Burke, a member of the British Parliament who turned out to be America's friend in England.

Messengers hurried southward to spread the news.

In February, 1775, General Gage sent British troops to Salem, Massachusetts, to get back the arms and supplies which the militia had stolen. They marched from Boston through an angry countryside to Salem only to discover—much to their surprise—that everything had been hidden. Finding nothing, they left.

Down south, in March, 1775, Patrick Henry stirred the hearts of his fellow Virginians when he cried out: "There is no longer any room for hope . . . The war is inevitable—and let it come! I repeat it . . . let it come!

"Gentlemen may cry peace, peace! But there is no peace. The war has actually begun! The next gale that sweeps from the north will bring to our ears the

17

clash of resounding arms! Our brethren are already in the field! Why stand we here idle? What is it that gentlemen wish? What would they have? Is life so dear, or peace so sweet, as to be purchased at the price of chains and slavery? Forbid it, Almighty God! I know not what course others may take, but as for me, give me liberty or give me death!"

Things to Remember about Chapter 2

Meanings of Words and Phrases

Intolerable: Unbearable, hard to live under.

Physical force: The power of one's body.

Rebellion: Organized resistance to the government.

Defy: To oppose; to act against.

Unite: To bring together.

Continental Congress: Called "Continental" because it represented the colonies on the continent of North America.

Declaration: A public announcement.

Cancel: To do away with.

Provincial: Local—that is, belonging to a province or state, a part of a country.

Militia: Troops of citizens legally armed in an emergency.

Year of decision: The deadline the Continental Congress gave the British to cancel the Intolerable Acts.

Cannon: Guns too big for one man to carry.

Ammunition: Arms or weapons, such as guns.

Code: A system of principles or laws.

Check Your Memory

1. How were the people of Massachusetts punished by the Intolerable Acts? (See page 13.)

2. Which three colonies were hurt most by the Quebec Act? What did they lose? (See page 13.)

3. What three important actions did the First Continental Congress take? (See page 13.)

4. What did Edmund Burke point out in his speech? (See page 17.)

Projects

1. Pretend that you were living in colonial times and keeping a diary. Write about the exciting things you would have seen if you had been (1) a British soldier in Boston; (2) a member of the First Continental Congress; and (3) a member of the Committee of Safety.

Projects

Coming Up in Chapter 3

2. Prepare and give a short speech which might have been made by George Washington, Patrick Henry, or John Hancock.

Paul Revere's ride . . . The Minutemen at Lexington and Concord . . . The Battle of Bunker Hill.

Questions for Your Classroom Discussions

1. Do you believe that it was right for the Committee of Safety to steal weapons from the British? Justify your answer.

2. If you had lived in the colonies in the 1700's, would you have remained loyal to King George III? Have a debate with classmates. Choose up sides pro and con.

Patrick Henry had acquired a name for himself as a speaker in the Virginia House of Burgesses. He stirred his fellow Virginians with such words as "Give me liberty or give me death!"

No one expected a battle when 700 British soldiers marched into Lexington, Massachusetts, on April 19, 1775. The redcoats were there to capture Sam Adams and John Hancock and to destroy the patriots' ammunition. The British were surprised when 70 Minutemen in an open field turned out to have guns. Among them was a freed black named Salem Poor (seen in the center of this picture). No one knows who fired the first shot, but the British were forced to march on to Concord. Eight Minutemen were killed and 10 wounded. It turned out to be the first battle in the Revolutionary War.

Chapter 3

The Road to Revolution

British General Gage had listened for 11 months to the heart-beat of rebellion. His spies gave him information almost every day. His desk was filled with "secret" papers from the Massachusetts Committee of Safety. Carefully listed were the arms and supplies that the colonists had hidden at Concord. In April, 1775, the General was ordered by the King to stop the colonial revolt in any way he could.

But the colonists knew as much about the General's plans as he did. Sharp eyes had watched rowboats gathering around British ships in Boston Harbor. Sharp ears had heard that British troops were getting ready to fight. Word came that British officers in disguise had been wandering about the highways. General Gage was out

to grab the arms and supplies at Concord! Besides, he was planning to capture Sam Adams and John Hancock, who were then hiding at Lexington.

On the evening of April 18, 1775, when Gage was all set to move, the Committee of Safety went into action. It asked all patriots with fast horses to act as messengers to warn the countryside. One of the patriots was Paul Revere, a metal worker who took to his horse and began what was later known as the

Paul Revere starting out on his famous "Midnight Ride" to warn the patriots that the British were coming.

From "Coinometry" (Sterling Publishing Co.)

A poem written by Ralph Waldo Emerson says: "The embattled farmers stood, and fired the shot heard round the world." This picture shows how the farmers in their farm clothes fought from behind trees and rocks.

famous "midnight ride." Riding hard and fast, Revere, helped by other messengers, managed to warn Adams, Hancock, and colonists in all towns around Boston: "The British are coming!"

When the British reached Lexington, on April 19, 1775, they found a brave band of Minutemen (including one freed black named Salem Poor) blocking their way on the village green. A British officer cried, "Disperse (scatter), ye rebels, disperse!"

Someone fired a shot from behind a stone wall. Firing then broke out all over. By the time the Minutemen had been scat-

tered, they had left eight of their own dead on the road. Adams and Hancock, on seeing the British arrive, had hurried across the fields, with Adams yelling, "This is a glorious day for America!" It was what he had been wishing for—a bloody fight that would lead to independence from England.

The British continued their march to Concord, where, as in the words of the New England poet, Ralph Waldo Emerson:

"... the embattled farmers stood, and fired the shot heard round the world."

The British had to retreat

Ethan Allen and his Green Mountain Boys arrived at Fort Ticonderoga in the middle of the night and found the defenders in their night clothes.

before the day was over. Some 1,800 British regulars had met some 4,000 American farmers and had been driven back to Boston. The Americans had lost altogether 49 dead, and 46 more were wounded or missing. The British had lost 65 dead and 173 more were wounded or missing.

Within one month, Ethan Allen and 83 men from New Hampshire—the "Green Mountain Boys"—captured the British forts at Ticonderoga and Crown Point on Lake Champlain in New York. Most welcome of all to colonists' ears was the news that arms and supplies from the captured forts were on their way

After the Battle of Lexington, the British went on to Concord and then had to withdraw when 4,000 farmers and other patriots opened fire at them.

News of the Battles of Lexington and Concord was carried to New York by a horseman seen here at The Bowery and Broadway. The New Yorkers had just left Sunday church.

to the militia who were expecting more trouble in Boston.

While all America was buzzing with the news of Lexington and Concord, the Second Continental Congress met at Philadelphia. Some of the delegates (especially Sam Adams, Patrick Henry, and Benjamin Franklin) were now ready to take "radical" or rebellious action—to declare American independence, seize British officials, and ask France and Spain for help in fighting the English. Most of the other delegates, however, were more "conservative" and against breaking all ties with Great Britain.

The conservatives won. A letter was sent to King George III, telling him that the colonists had no idea of separating from the mother country. But to this plea for peace the delegates added a strong message which made it clear that they would fight tyranny with force if necessary.

To show that they meant business, they appointed George Washington commander-in-chief of the Continental Army. The armed colonists around Boston became, in name at least, an army.

The rebellion spread to the other colonies. In most cases, the militia forced royal governors to seek safety on British ships. But the four Middle Colonies— New York, New Jersey, Pennsylvania, and Maryland—told their delegates in the Congress to hold out against independence.

Before General Washington reached Boston to take command of the Continental Army, blood had flowed again. General Gage —helped by Generals John Burgoyne, William Howe, and Henry Clinton—attacked the New Englanders who were dug in at Charlestown, overlooking Boston Harbor. In three bold attacks, the British tried to drive the Americans from Breed's Hill. (When you visit

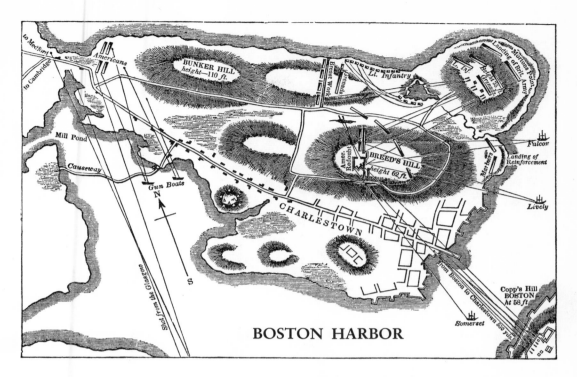

BOSTON HARBOR

Boston, your guide will tell you that the monument on Bunker Hill really belongs on Breed's Hill, where the battle was actually fought.) It was a victory for the redcoats, but

In even rows, the British marched from their ships up Breed's Hill, where they were met with gunfire from the patriots.

At the Battle of "Bunker Hill," Peter Salem, a black Minuteman, killed a British officer.

From the "International Library of Negro Life and History" published for the Association for the Study of Negro Life and History by the Publishers Company, Inc, Washington, D.C.

a costly one. They lost 1,054 dead and wounded out of a total of 2,200 troops; the colonists lost 441 dead and wounded out of a total of 3,200 troops. Among the Minutemen who lived through the battle was a black slave named Peter Salem, who won his freedom.

"A dear victory," wrote British General Clinton—"another such would have ruined us."

Angered by the news from Breed's Hill, King George III announced that a general rebellion existed in America. "An all-out effort should be made to stop the revolt and bring the traitors justice," he announced. He also hired 10,000 German mercenary soldiers, called Hessians, to help the British Army force the colonists into obeying the British Crown.

Englishman Edmund Burke, America's friend—still trying to prevent a war—in November, 1775, made a peace proposal to the House of Commons. The House turned it down by a vote of two to one. Parliament, in turn, passed an Act which stopped all trade with the 13 colonies. This new law also declared all colonial ships were "lawful prize" (free for the taking) and their crews subject to "compulsory service" (forced labor) in the British navy.

Late in 1775, Washington ordered an expedition to invade Canada. He wanted to take it away from the British and prevent an attack from the north. Richard Montgomery, leading 1,000 New Englanders, easily captured Montreal. Soon, General Benedict Arnold, marching through Maine with 600 patriots, joined Montgomery near Quebec. The two generals intended to take the city, but they were beaten. Montgomery, badly wounded, fell dead.

General Washington, attacking the British in Boston, received the bad news in January, 1776. To him, it was all too clear that the British now had control of

Canada, which the patriots wanted so badly. But Washington still would not give up. He and his men fought on to take Dorchester Heights near Boston, forcing General Howe to leave Massachusetts.

Things to Remember about Chapter 3

Meanings of Words and Phrases

Revolt: To break away from or rise against authority, as by open rebellion.

Disguise: Dress to look like someone else.

Volunteers: People who offer their services.

Disperse: To go in different directions.

Radical action: Sweeping changes in government with the least delay.

Conservative: A person who believes in leaving things as they are.

Traitor: One who rebels against his country.

Mercenary: A soldier who fights for anyone who pays him.

Hessian: A German soldier hired by the British.

Compulsory service: Forced service in armed forces.

Expedition: A journey made for some special purpose, as of war or exploration.

Check Your Memory

1. Why did General Gage have British troops march on Lexington? on Concord? (See page 21.)

2. Why was Paul Revere's ride important? (See pages 21-22.)

Check Your Memory

3. Why did Samuel Adams call April 19, 1775, a glorious day for America? (See page 22.)

4. What did Ethan Allen's raid achieve? (See page 23.)

5. What did the "radicals" in the Second Continental Congress want to do? (See page 24.)

6. What did King George III do following the Battle of Bunker (Breed's) Hill? (See page 26.)

Projects

1. Read the biographies of some of these New England leaders: (1) Samuel Adams, (2) Paul Revere, (3) John Hancock, and (4) Ethan Allen. Recommend the book you like best to a friend.

2. Read about the Minutemen in *Pioneers and Patriots* by Lavinia Dobler and E. A. Toppin.

3. Check your map to find Concord, Lexington, Boston, Philadelphia, and New Hampshire.

Coming Up in Chapter 4

Thomas Paine's *Common Sense* . . . The Declaration of Independence.

Questions for Your Classroom Discussions

1. Do you believe that colonial independence was a necessary step? Explain your answer.

2. In your opinion, why were the colonists most opposed to strong British control?

3. How did colonial armed resistance grow into an organized rebellion?

The Declaration of Independence

Seven months before the famous Fourth of July in 1776, there appeared in the colonies a "best-seller" pamphlet called *Common Sense*. It was written by Thomas Paine, a political writer and a friend of Benjamin Franklin. Paine, then in his 30's, had arrived from England less than two years before. He had once wanted to become a sailor, but gave up the idea when he found that he liked writing more than sailing. A rebel by nature, he had managed to put into *Common Sense* the thoughts of every American who wanted independence.

When Tom Paine wrote his pamphlet, "Common Sense," he had been in America only two years. He put into words what many Americans were thinking about their independence.

Paine's arguments were powerful. Non-importation of British goods had failed, hurting America more than it did England. To obtain money for arms and supplies, America would *have* to trade with other nations. Peace was no longer possible. There was no certainty that Parliament would not again try to limit colonial liberties. Complete independence was the only answer, Paine wrote. An independent America could trade with the whole world, make what she liked, and stay out of Old World fights. King George III had not kept his word with Americans to protect their rights. So he gave up his right to their loyalty.

"Common Sense" was bought by 120,000 Americans in three months. In it, Paine said, "It is absurd that an island should rule a continent."

Stirred by Paine's arguments, more and more colonists began to want independence. In a letter to a friend, General Washington wrote that "the sound reasoning of *Common Sense* made one easily see why many Americans wanted separation."

The movement for independence got a really strong boost in the Second Continental Congress. Richard Henry Lee, a Virginia delegate (later known as Light-Horse Harry), introduced his famous resolution declaring that "these United Colonies are, and of right ought to be, free and independent states."

John Adams, in a letter to his wife, Abigail, wrote, ". . . independence rolls in on us like a torrent."

To explain why Americans were rebelling, and what new form of government they were planning, the Congress appointed Thomas Jefferson and four others to prepare and write a Declaration of Independence. Jefferson was a master of many things, an excellent writer, and full of ideas. At the time, he was 33 years old and a gentleman farmer, with a plantation in Virginia, called Monticello. Besides being a lawyer, he was a scientist and inventor. Later, he was a founder of the University of Virginia.

Of the four men who were appointed to help Jefferson, Benjamin Franklin was the most important. As we know, he was a Philadelphian, a printer and book lover, an inventor and scientist. Seventy years old at the time, he had performed a famous experiment — drawing lightning from the clouds with a kite and a key. His ideas generally agreed with Jefferson's.

John Adams, 41 years old, was also well known. A cousin of Sam Adams, he was a graduate of Harvard, and a leading Boston lawyer. He too was a great reader of books.

The other two men on the

(Above) Ben Franklin had become famous as a scientist because of an experiment he made in June, 1752. He showed that lightning and electricity were the same thing by flying a kite with a key at the end of the string into a thunderstorm. This discovery led to his invention of lightning rods to protect homes.

(Right) Ben Franklin and John Adams discussing the writing of the Declaration of Independence with Tom Jefferson.

Here is the gathering of the patriot leaders in Independence Hall, Philadelphia, as they signed the Declaration of Independence. John Hancock was the first to sign.

committee were hardly known. One was Roger Sherman, 55, an assistant governor of Connecticut, and a treasurer of Yale College.

Robert R. Livingston, from New York, just 30, was a good speaker, a practicing lawyer, and a graduate of Kings College, later Columbia.

Tom Jefferson was the one chosen to write the Declaration. He began by making a long list of complaints about King George. Adding a few ideas about liberty, he then described the patriots' feelings. The other four men argued with him over a word here and there, an idea or two, but added only a few ideas of their own. Still, it was not

complete. On June 28, 1776, the committee presented the document to Congress.

Some interesting changes were then made during a debate by the whole Congress. Jefferson had included in his bitter attack on the King: "The Virginia Assembly should not be stopped from passing laws against the African slave trade." The South Carolina and Rhode Island delegates said, "No," and it was taken out.

Jefferson's objection to the use of Hessians to put down the rebellion had read, "Scots and Hessians," since Scots had been sent by the King to Boston. At that, a New Jersey delegate jumped to his feet and said he

In CONGRESS. July 4, 1776.

The unanimous Declaration of the thirteen united States of America.

When in the Course of human events, it becomes necessary for one people to dissolve the political bands which have connected them with another, and to assume among the powers of the earth, the separate and equal station to which the Laws of Nature and of Nature's God entitle them, a decent respect to the opinions of mankind requires that they should declare the causes which impel them to the separation.

We hold these truths to be self-evident, that all men are created equal, that they are endowed by their Creator with certain unalienable Rights, that among these are Life, Liberty and the pursuit of Happiness.—That to secure these rights, Governments are instituted among Men, deriving their just powers from the consent of the governed,—That whenever any Form of Government becomes destructive of these ends, it is the Right of the People to alter or to abolish it, and to institute new Government, laying its foundation on such principles and organizing its powers in such form, as to them shall seem most likely to effect their Safety and Happiness. Prudence, indeed, will dictate that Governments long established should not be changed for light and transient causes; and accordingly all experience hath shewn, that mankind are more disposed to suffer, while evils are sufferable, than to right themselves by abolishing the forms to which they are accustomed. But when a long train of abuses and usurpations, pursuing invariably the same Object evinces a design to reduce them under absolute Despotism, it is their right, it is their duty, to throw off such Government, and to provide new Guards for their future security.—Such has been the patient sufferance of these Colonies; and such is now the necessity which constrains them to alter their former Systems of Government. The history of the present King of Great Britain is a history of repeated injuries and usurpations, all having in direct object the establishment of an absolute Tyranny over these States. To prove this, let Facts be submitted to a candid world.

He has refused his Assent to Laws, the most wholesome and necessary for the public good.

He has forbidden his Governors to pass Laws of immediate and pressing importance, unless suspended in their operation till his Assent should be obtained; and when so suspended, he has utterly neglected to attend to them.

He has refused to pass other Laws for the accommodation of large districts of people, unless those people would relinquish the right of Representation in the Legislature, a right inestimable to them and formidable to tyrants only.

He has called together legislative bodies at places unusual, uncomfortable, and distant from the depository of their public Records, for the sole purpose of fatiguing them into compliance with his measures.

He has dissolved Representative Houses repeatedly, for opposing with manly firmness his invasions on the rights of the people.

He has refused for a long time, after such dissolutions, to cause others to be elected; whereby the Legislative powers, incapable of Annihilation, have returned to the People at large for their exercise; the State remaining in the mean time exposed to all the dangers of invasion from without, and convulsions within.

He has endeavoured to prevent the population of these States; for that purpose obstructing the Laws for Naturalization of Foreigners; refusing to pass others to encourage their migrations hither, and raising the conditions of new Appropriations of Lands.

He has obstructed the Administration of Justice, by refusing his Assent to Laws for establishing Judiciary powers.

He has made Judges dependent on his Will alone, for the tenure of their offices, and the amount and payment of their salaries.

He has erected a multitude of New Offices, and sent hither swarms of Officers to harrass our people, and eat out their substance.

He has kept among us, in times of peace, Standing Armies without the Consent of our legislatures.

He has affected to render the Military independent of and superior to the Civil power.

He has combined with others to subject us to a jurisdiction foreign to our constitution, and unacknowledged by our laws; giving his Assent to their Acts of pretended Legislation:

For Quartering large bodies of armed troops among us:—For protecting them, by a mock Trial, from punishment for any Murders which they should commit on the Inhabitants of these States:—For cutting off our Trade with all parts of the world:—For imposing Taxes on us without our Consent:—For depriving us in many cases, of the benefits of Trial by Jury:—For transporting us beyond Seas to be tried for pretended offences:—For abolishing the free System of English Laws in a neighbouring Province, establishing therein an Arbitrary government, and enlarging its Boundaries so as to render it at once an example and fit instrument for introducing the same absolute rule into these Colonies:—For taking away our Charters, abolishing our most valuable Laws, and altering fundamentally the Forms of our Governments:—For suspending our own Legislatures, and declaring themselves invested with power to legislate for us in all cases whatsoever.

He has abdicated Government here, by declaring us out of his Protection and waging War against us.

He has plundered our seas, ravaged our Coasts, burnt our towns, and destroyed the lives of our people.

He is at this time transporting large Armies of foreign Mercenaries to compleat the works of death, desolation and tyranny, already begun with circumstances of Cruelty & perfidy scarcely paralleled in the most barbarous ages, and totally unworthy the Head of a civilized nation.

He has constrained our fellow Citizens taken Captive on the high Seas to bear Arms against their Country, to become the executioners of their friends and Brethren, or to fall themselves by their Hands.

He has excited domestic insurrections amongst us, and has endeavoured to bring on the inhabitants of our frontiers, the merciless Indian Savages, whose known rule of warfare, is an undistinguished destruction of all ages, sexes and conditions.

In every stage of these Oppressions We have Petitioned for Redress in the most humble terms: Our repeated Petitions have been answered only by repeated injury. A Prince, whose character is thus marked by every act which may define a Tyrant, is unfit to be the ruler of a free people.

Nor have We been wanting in attentions to our British brethren. We have warned them from time to time of attempts by their legislature to extend an unwarrantable jurisdiction over us. We have reminded them of the circumstances of our emigration and settlement here. We have appealed to their native justice and magnanimity, and we have conjured them by the ties of our common kindred to disavow these usurpations, which, would inevitably interrupt our connections and correspondence. They too have been deaf to the voice of justice and of consanguinity. We must, therefore, acquiesce in the necessity, which denounces our Separation, and hold them, as we hold the rest of mankind, Enemies in War, in Peace Friends.

We, therefore, the Representatives of the united States of America, in General Congress, Assembled, appealing to the Supreme Judge of the world for the rectitude of our intentions, do, in the Name, and by Authority of the good People of these Colonies, solemnly publish and declare, That these United Colonies are, and of Right ought to be Free and Independent States; that they are Absolved from all Allegiance to the British Crown, and that all political connection between them and the State of Great Britain, is and ought to be totally dissolved; and that as Free and Independent States, they have full Power to levy War, conclude Peace, contract Alliances, establish Commerce, and to do all other Acts and Things which Independent States may of right do.—And for the support of this Declaration, with a firm reliance on the protection of Divine Providence, we mutually pledge to each other our Lives, our Fortunes and our sacred Honor.

The Declaration of Independence.

---

would not have Scotland insulted. So "Scots" was taken out.

Finally, the Declaration was adopted by Congress on July 4, 1776. It was signed first by John Hancock in his beautiful large handwriting, and then by delegates from all the colonies. It was read from the balcony of Philadelphia's Independence Hall on July 8.

Most of the Americans, now

In this room in Independence Hall, Philadelphia, the Declaration of Independence was signed on July 4, 1776. This is the way the room looks today. Visitors are welcome.

Independence Hall, Philadelphia, as it looks today from the outside. In the tower is the famous Liberty Bell.

called patriots or Whigs, greeted the news of the Declaration of Independence with great celebration. Cannon were fired. Bells rang. People sang and danced around bonfires. Happily for them, the long days of waiting were over. They were now citizens of the United States of America.

Among those celebrating was a freed Boston slave named Phillis Wheatley. Her book of poems published in 1773 did much to inspire the patriots.

Some other Americans, called Loyalists or Tories, wanted no part of the celebration. Still loyal to King George III, they sat quietly behind locked doors and barred windows. To them, the bonfires were a sign of terror. They had already known violence and knew what to expect—neighbor against neighbor, house burnings, beatings, and escape to Canada, the British West Indies, or England.

The rest of the people did not take sides. They were neither patriots nor Loyalists, and did not care one way or another about America's independence.

The Declaration did much to win public support for the Americans in Europe. Each of the listed complaints in the Declaration was directed against one man—King George III. "He has refused . . . he has forbidden . . . he has obstructed . . . he has plundered . . . he has excited. . . ." In contrast,

Phillis Wheatley, born in Africa and owned by a Boston tailor, won her freedom from slavery by writing patriotic poetry.

Jefferson tried to picture the patriots as patient, law-abiding, long-suffering citizens. "We have warned . . . we have reminded . . . we have appealed . . . we have been wanting . . . we have petitioned. . . ."

Going further, the Declaration clearly and simply explained what we now call democracy. As Jefferson described it: ". . . All men are created equal." (Could he have been thinking of black people when he wrote this?) "They are endowed by their Creator with certain unalienable rights" (rights which cannot be taken away by the government or even by the people themselves). "Among these are life, liberty, and the pursuit of happiness."

Jefferson explained that men

35

needed a government that got its "just powers from the consent of the governed." As he and his fellow patriots saw it, the people had the *right* to change or end a tyrannical government. Besides, they had the *right* to revolt against the British and rule themselves.

Beyond this, the Declaration announced that war existed. As Thomas Paine had argued in *Common Sense*, this announcement gave Americans the advantages of being an independent nation. But if the patriots lost in their fight for independence, they could be accused of treason and be sentenced to death by the British.

So it was no empty phrase that Jefferson wrote: ". . . We mutually pledge to each other our lives, our fortunes, and our sacred honor."

Things to Remember about Chapter 4

Meanings of Words and Phrases

Loyalist: A person who is loyal, in this case, loyal to the king.

Tory: Same as Loyalist. The Tory political party in Great Britain believed in full power for the king. For this reason, Americans loyal to the king were often called Tories.

Obstruct: To block or prevent.

Plunder: To rob or take wrongfully; to loot.

Law-abiding: Obeying the law.

Petition: To ask for.

Endow: To give something to a person.

Unalienable rights: Rights which cannot be taken away from the people by the government or even by the people themselves.

Pledge: A promise or agreement.

Check Your Memory

1. What pamphlet helped many Americans to decide in favor of independence? (See page 29.)

2. Why was the Declaration of Independence written? (See page 30.)

3. Who were the five members of the committee that drew up the Declaration of Independence? (See page 30.)

Projects

1. Read and discuss with your teacher the original document of the Declaration of Independence. See if you can explain the important points to your younger brother or sister. Also explain it to a first-grade class in your school.

2. Make a poster that could have been used to influence the

Richard Allen was a black minister who preached from a church near Independence Hall in Philadelphia. His congregation included both white and black people. A scene from the inside of his church is shown on the front cover of this book.

colonists to rebel against Great Britain in 1776.

3. Go to your school library and see what you can learn about Phillis Wheatley.

Coming Up in Chapter 5

Army problems . . . Black patriots . . . The war at sea.

Questions for Your Classroom Discussions

1. Do you agree with the saying "the pen is mightier than the sword"? If so, what person's writings would you use for an example?

2. If you had been one of the American colonists in 1776, how would you have reacted to the Declaration of Independence? Describe your feelings.

3. Do you believe that Thomas Jefferson was thinking of black people when he wrote "all men are created equal"? What do we mean by human rights?

4. The Declaration of Independence has been described as the "birth certificate" of the United States of America. Explain what this statement means.

In the beginning, American troops had no uniforms and looked no better than a poorly dressed crowd of farmers.

Chapter 5

America under Arms

The Declaration of Independence had no sooner been signed than most of Washington's army wanted to go home. They were farmers and their crops needed harvesting. They half expected the King to give up when he read Jefferson's ringing words. Many Americans did not care one way or another about independence, and did not support the army. Many Loyalists were openly against independence and especially the war. But, the fighting went on.

Few patriots paid much attention to John Adams when he said, "We shall have a long and bloody war." Most Americans thought the war would be over in a year. The British, even more hopeful, thought it would be over in a few months. If the Americans had known how long and difficult the war would be, they might have made Congress give up the fight. If the British had known how stubborn General Washington would be, they might have given Congress everything it asked for—freedom from British taxes and self-government.

General Washington had served with British troops in the French and Indian War and respected them as fighters. To make the Continental Army equal to that of the British was, indeed, a difficult task.

Americans hated the idea of standing armies. Under the colonial system they had been asked to serve only short enlistments. Most men were against signing up now with the Continental Army for even a year. Few, if any, were willing to re-enlist. Southerners did not want to go to New England to fight. New Englanders did not want to go south to fight. No money was given to families whose men were in service. No pensions were paid to families whose men were killed in action.

In the beginning, American troops were little better than a poorly dressed crowd of farmers. A Frenchman, watching them march, described them as being "miserable in appearance." Army

Haym Salomon, a Polish Jew who had come to America only four years before the Declaration of Independence, gave $350,000 of his own earnings to help the new nation.

spirit or morale was low. The Army lacked regular uniforms, awards, and decorations. The Purple Heart, created by General Washington to honor men for outstanding military service, was not awarded until 1782. There was little or no money to pay salaries.

Things certainly would have been worse than they were, if Congress had not received $350,000 from Haym Salomon. A Polish Jew, Salomon had come to America only four years before the Declaration of Independence. In New York, he had been sent to prison by the British as a spy, but had escaped to Philadelphia, where he made a great deal of money as a banker. It was his own money that he "lent" to the new government, and the loan was never repaid.

It was not until the end of 1776 that Congress gave General Washington the power to make all promotions up to and including colonel. Officers' arguments, especially those of generals, gave Washington more trouble than the discipline of regular troops.

General Washington had many friends in Congress, some of whom he had worked with in the Virginia House of Burgesses. They knew he was both capable and reliable. But many of his fellow officers were not. Some who showed real ability were badly treated by Congress. General Nathanael Greene, one of the best officers, was passed

over when it came to promotion. The fearless Benedict Arnold was also ignored. He filled up with hidden anger, and ended as a traitor, a general on the British side. A small group of officers even went so far as to try to get George Washington replaced by General Horatio Gates.

Sadly in need of military advice, the Americans were glad to welcome foreign volunteers.

Pulaski

Kosciusko

von Steuben

Lafayette

Foreign soldiers who fought on America's side in the Revolution have been honored on United States stamps and coins.

German Baron Friedrich W. A. von Steuben did a great deal to organize and drill the troops. Polish Count Casimir Pulaski gave his life in the Battle of Savannah. Thaddeus Kosciusko, another Pole, taught the Americans about artillery, the use of cannon and large guns. French Marquis de Lafayette became a close friend of Washington, and served with honor in the

41

Virginia campaign that ended the war.

Turning down black men for military service was the rule. It seemed not to matter that blacks had fought in the French and Indian War. Nor did it seem to matter that Crispus Attucks had sparked the patriots' cause by giving his life in the Boston Massacre. Blacks who had fought at Lexington and Concord and at Breed's Hill found out that their services were neither asked for nor wanted.

The military leaders twice turned down the idea of using blacks—slave or free—as soldiers. General Washington gave an order in 1775 forbidding recruiting officers to enlist "Negroes, boys unable to bear arms, and old men. . . ." When free black soldiers came to Washington and protested the discrimination against them, the general backed off. He permitted the enlistment of free blacks. He hastened to add, however, that if Congress disapproved, he would put a stop to it.

But as things turned out, the racial policy of the Continental Army was in the end largely dictated by what the British did. In the first year of the war, Governor John Murray Dunmore of Virginia, a Loyalist, promised freedom to all blacks who fought on the British side. The Virginia slaveholders were alarmed that they would lose their slaves. General Washington was worried

British officers trying to force secrets from a black patriot.

A statue of King George III in New York City, which had been erected only a few years before, was torn down by patriots on July 9, 1776, five days after the signing of the Declaration of Independence.

that the Loyalist strength would increase. In 1778, Thomas Jefferson estimated that at least 30,000 Virginia slaves had run away.

Finally, General Washington and Congress were forced to change their minds. By the end of the war, some 5,000 blacks had fought for independence and won their freedom. But Paul Cuffe, a Massachusetts sailor who later became a shipbuilder, and other black leaders realized that not all blacks would be free. They told the patriot leaders that they knew the benefits gained from the American Revolution were for whites, not blacks.

A three-pence bill printed by Ben Franklin for King George III in 1764.

The Continental Dollar, very hard to find these days, was first issued in 1776, the year of the Declaration of Independence.

At sea, the British navy might have done better, if France had not stepped in. A tight blockade of the North American coast was not possible in those days of slow sailing ships. But the British navy, with 28 warships in ports between Halifax, Nova Scotia, and Florida, was strong enough to keep the narrow trade routes open. This made it possible for the British to move troops by sea from England to America, or from one American port to another.

General Washington organized what was called the army's salt-water navy, which was made up of small ships. In addition, there was also a fresh-water navy on Lake Champlain, which kept the British from attacking New York in 1776.

No less than six states—Massachusetts and Pennsylvania, Maryland, Virginia, and the Carolinas—had navies of their own to guard rivers or search for prizes off shore. Congress and most of the states hired patriot privateers (privately owned armed ships) to upset enemy shipping.

Congress tried to organize a navy in 1775. As Samuel Chase of Maryland said, "It was the maddest idea in the world to think of building an American fleet."

Meanwhile, Congress had approved the building of 12 frigates (fast, heavily armed ships), which it expected to be ready for sea in three months. Four of the frigates were blown up to prevent their falling into enemy hands. Frigates *Warren* and *Raleigh* were ready for duty in the spring of 1776, but the *Warren*, together with the *Providence*, was trapped in

A naval battle fought by America's fresh-water navy on Lake Champlain in 1776.

The "Ranger," commanded by John Paul Jones, was the first ship flying the Stars and Stripes to receive a gun salute from the ships of a foreign nation. It happened off the coast of France in 1778, as pictured here.

Narragansett Bay by the British for two years. The *Raleigh*, short of men, never left port until 1777, and was taken by the British within a year. The *Virginia*, built in Baltimore, was captured even before leaving Chesapeake Bay. The *Randolph*, without a crew, remained in Charleston for months, and in her first fight, she blew up. The *Hancock* was taken by the British and renamed the *Iris*. All of the earlier ships had been captured or destroyed by the end of 1779. At the war's end, the navy had only one or two small ships.

The real naval victories of the war, for America, were made by John Paul Jones or by the Royal Navy of France. A Scot by birth, John Paul (who named himself Jones) was a sailor from the age of 12. He fell in love with America when he first landed at the age of 13. From merchant ships, it was a short step to ships of war.

When he was named a captain, John Paul Jones captured 16 prizes in 47 days on a cruise to the West Indies. Then he captured a number of British ships carrying coal from Nova Scotia and freed 100 Americans working as prisoners in the mines. Later he sailed to France to tell the news of American victories on land. Sailing along the north coast of England he seized a port, knocked out its guns and burned some ships. He even captured 40-gun and 20-gun warships, far superior to his own. But you will learn more about him in Chapter 7.

Things to Remember about Chapter 5

Meanings of Words and Phrases

Enlistment: The length of time for which one agrees to serve in the armed forces of his country.

Morale: The mental attitude or spirit, good or bad, that one has toward the things he must do.

Discrimination: Favoring one group of people over another, because of race, color, or religion.

Blockade: Closing a port, harbor, or coastline to prevent enemy ships sailing in.

Privateer: A privately owned armed ship hired by a government to fight or bother enemy shipping.

Frigate: A fast sailing ship, heavily armed.

Check Your Memory

1. Why was the Revolutionary War unpopular and why did so many colonists object to military service? (See page 39.)

2. Why was it so difficult for General Washington to organize the Continental Army? (See page 39.)

3. What did the British do that made it necessary for the Continental Army to change its racial policy? (See page 43.)

Projects

1. List the advantages that the British had over the Americans in 1775, when the Revolution began.

2. Read *John Paul Jones, Fighting Sailor* by Armstrong Perry.

3. Find out what you can about Paul Cuffe.

Coming Up in Chapter 6

Americans versus the British . . . The greatness of General Washington . . . American victories.

Questions for Your Classroom Discussions

1. Do you believe that the American Revolution was necessary? Justify your answer.

2. If you had been a black soldier in the Continental Army, what argument would you have given General Washington against racial discrimination?

3. Suppose the Americans had been able to build and keep a navy during the Revolutionary War. How might history have been changed?

When General Washington wanted to take his soldiers from Long Island across to Manhattan Island, he found this British fleet blocking his way in lower New York Harbor.

New York Public Library

Chapter 6

The War in the North

General Washington had 20,000 patriots guarding New York City in April, 1776. But he found that a British army of 30,000 men had landed on Staten Island under General Howe. More than 100 British ships rested at anchor in New York Harbor.

Washington had but one way out. That was to move as many men as he could across the East River to Brooklyn Heights, where his guns could control the harbor. But Howe took Washington by surprise by moving in behind him, from the Long Island side, at the end of the summer of 1776. This Battle of Long Island came close to ending the war right then and there.

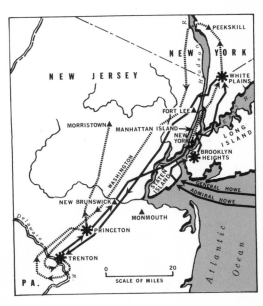

This is the route that General Washington took his army along to get away from the British in 1776 after having lost the Battle of Long Island.

Much of the fighting in the Battle of Long Island took place in Brooklyn. Here the smoke of battle rises around the old Cortelyou house.

One of the spies who had been sent to Long Island to get information for Washington from behind the British lines was Nathan Hale. He was disguised as a Dutch schoolteacher. When he was about to return with the information, he was captured and hanged at once. His last words were: "I only regret that I have but one life to give for my country."

Washington now chose to move his troops to low, flat ground, instead of fighting from Brooklyn Heights. The British were used to open-field warfare, the Americans were not. Howe led his Britishers well. Washington lost over 1,000 men killed, wounded, and captured.

But Howe failed to give chase, letting Washington make a safe retreat. Nine thousand men—

One of Washington's generals named Sullivan led his troops through Flatbush Pass in Brooklyn when getting away from the British.

When the American soldiers retreated from Long Island, there was great disorder. However, Washington managed to get most of his troops across to Manhattan.

As the patriot Nathan Hale was about to be hanged, he uttered the famous words, "I only regret that I have but one life to give for my country!"

Hamilton's cannon in action at the Battle of White Plains is shown on this stamp.

along with cannon, horses, and supplies—were ferried across the East River to Manhattan in less than 12 hours. Skillful retreats do not win wars. This one, however, saved an army from being totally destroyed and let America continue the war for independence.

Washington knew now that New York City was lost. So he fled northward, trying to protect the rear of his army against a British naval attack from the East River. At White Plains, where Alexander Hamilton, who

In retreating northward, General Washington stopped from time to time to fight the British. Here, he is at what is now known as Washington Heights, at the northern end of Manhattan Island, looking across to the Palisades.

was then only 19, was in charge of one of the cannon, Washington's forces were beaten again. Meanwhile, other parts of his army suffered defeats in New Jersey. Washington managed somehow to reorganize his army at Hackensack. From here, he led his tired, unhappy men south across New Jersey to the Delaware River. Luckily, Howe did not move in to finish him off.

When the British entered Philadelphia, the Continental Congress hurriedly moved to Baltimore and met in this house.

By late October, 1776, Washington's position was becoming serious. Winter was on the way. The Americans had lost many men and supplies. Defeat seemed certain. The army was rapidly melting away. Soldiers by the hundreds were returning to their homes.

In early December, 1776, Washington led his remaining troops across the Delaware River into Pennsylvania. They were just a jump ahead of the redcoats who were chasing them. There was no way of keeping the British out of Philadelphia. The Second Continental Congress fled hastily to Baltimore. "I must have more men and supplies," Washington wrote, "or I think the fight will be pretty well over." One thing he *had* gotten was a flag—a red, white and blue flag much like our

General Washington made a brilliant counterattack against the British on Christmas night, 1776. Flying his new flag, he and his men crossed the Delaware River and at Trenton surprised the Hessian army who were fighting for the British. (See the map on page 47.)

present Star-Spangled Banner. One of the stories about the flag handed down to us was that a woman named Betsy Ross sewed the new flag with her own hands, using a design given to her by General Washington. This is a charming legend, but it is not true.

Almost as if spurred on by his bad luck, George Washington now gathered his troops for a brilliant counterattack. Knowing that Howe's army was widely scattered, he recrossed the ice-filled Delaware River on the stormy Christmas night of 1776, with the new flag flying. Shortly after daybreak the Americans surprised some 1,300 Hessians at nearby Trenton. The Hessian commander was killed, and his men were taken prisoner. Among

Washington's men was a freed black man named Prince Whipple.

Following this victory, Washington moved north to Princeton where the patriots badly beat a British force. The general and his men were now too tired to go on, so Washington decided to spend the rest of the winter in the woods at Morristown. Anyway, they had chased the British out of New Jersey. And once again, the Americans dared hope that they would win the war.

The British, upset by their losses at Trenton and Princeton, hoped to end the war in 1777. General John Burgoyne had developed a master plan and the King had agreed to let him carry it out. A large British army, led by Burgoyne, was to

51

Hugh Mercer, an American General, was killed at the Battle of Princeton.

push southward from Canada along Lake Champlain. A small army, led by Colonel Barry St. Leger, was to push eastward from Lake Ontario through the Mohawk Valley of upper New York. Another large British army, led by General Howe, was to sail up the Hudson River from New York City to Albany. Together, the three armies were to crush between them any Americans that could be tricked into a fight with them. Also, this action would cut off New England from New York.

General Howe planned differently. He would finish off Philadelphia first. That would end the war. The British colonial secretary in London told Howe to go ahead, believing that the General could keep his date later with Burgoyne at Albany. So, on

July 4, 1777, Howe set sail from New York City with 15,000 men. His plan was to land near the head of Chesapeake Bay, and then march from there to Philadelphia.

To stop this army, Washington had 12,000 men, including militia. So few had uniforms that the General ordered each man to wear a sprig of green on his jacket as a symbol of hope. Clearly, Philadelphia could not be given up without a fight. The best thing that Washington could do was to delay the enemy.

Washington made his first stand on September 11 at Brandywine Creek. The Americans, no match for the British, lost 1,000 men killed and wounded. Howe, happy over his victory, went on to take Philadelphia. Still not satisfied, he sent a part of his army to the Delaware River to destroy two American forts.

On October 4, Washington made his second stand at Germantown, just north of Philadelphia. Howe was again victorious. The Americans lost another 1,000 men. Washington moved on to Valley Forge, where he and the rest of his army spent the winter. It was so cold and they had so little to eat that more than 3,000 men died.

When Benjamin Franklin, then the American Ambassador in Paris, heard that Howe had taken Philadelphia, he replied, "No, Philadelphia has taken Howe." And so it was, for Howe gave himself over to the delights of the city's Loyalist society and enjoyed himself.

The British campaign in New York that Burgoyne had so carefully planned now got under way without Howe and his army. Colonel St. Leger, as ordered, left Oswego, New York, and

This map shows the plans that were made for British General Howe and the moves he really made. Instead of going north to help Burgoyne at Saratoga, he went south and came back up through Chesapeake Bay. He met Washington at Brandywine and later Germantown, then went to Philadelphia while Washington went to Valley Forge.

Much of the fighting at the Battle of Germantown took place around the home of the Chew family.

General Nicholas Herkimer, when wounded, was propped up against a tree. In that way, he directed the Battle of Oriskany.

headed for the Mohawk Valley and Fort Stanwix, now Rome, New York. The British were promised a big turnout of Loyalists and Mohawk Indians. But there was a bigger turnout of patriots led by General Nicholas Herkimer. On August 7, 1777, St. Leger reached Fort Stanwix. Herkimer, on the way to the fort, was attacked by Mohawks and badly wounded.

A small army under Benedict Arnold, then a general under Washington, now marched up the Mohawk Valley to capture the fort back. Arnold wisely spread ghost stories, which caused the Mohawk Indians to run out on Colonel St. Leger, who then gave up the fight and headed for Canada.

Meanwhile, General Burgoyne was moving southward from Canada down the Lake Champlain trail. The General knew no more about this part of the American wilderness than did his superiors in London. To make things worse, his march was greatly slowed down by officers' wives, children, and loads of baggage. Finally, after weeks of marching, he reached Fort Ticonderoga on Lake Champlain, which he took after very little fighting. Then, his troubles really began.

Painting by John Trumbull, courtesy of Yale University Art Gallery

British General Burgoyne had to surrender to the American forces at Saratoga, New York. His fellow officers and their troops had failed to get to Saratoga in time for the big battle. (See the map on page 53.)

On August 11, at Bennington, Vermont, a group of Green Mountain Boys fell upon some 500 Hessians, whom Burgoyne had sent out for supplies, and killed them all. A few days before, General Burgoyne had received the sad news that Howe had gone to Philadelphia.

"I little knew," Burgoyne wrote, "that I would be left alone without help from New York." But he pushed on to Saratoga. There, he was greatly outnumbered by the Americans under Generals Horatio Gates and Benedict Arnold, and was stopped. While Gates was arguing about the Revolution in his tent with a captured British officer, Arnold led an excellently planned attack. On October 17, 1777, Burgoyne gave up.

Gates, as top commander, got all of the credit for the victory. Benedict Arnold, totally ignored, began to think that he would be better appreciated by the British than by the Americans.

The Battle of Saratoga was the turning point of the war. All the British forces in New York had been captured. Howe was left in Philadelphia, but Washington was camped just outside the city. The patriots had won some important victories, and their spirits were high. Unless more soldiers, many more, came from England, the patriots felt they could hold on until they won total victory.

Things to Remember about Chapter 6

Meanings of Words and Phrases

Retreat: To move back.

Counterattack: To change from moving back to moving forward.

Master plan: A large over-all campaign.

Symbol: A sign of any kind used to stand for something.

Turning point: The time when an important change takes place.

Check Your Memory

1. Why were General Washington's victories at Trenton and Princeton so important? (See page 51.)

2. What did General Howe do that led to General Burgoyne's defeat? (See pages 52-53.)

3. In what way was General Gates unfair to General Arnold? (See page 55.)

Projects

1. Investigate and write a short report on the financial problems of the Revolution.

2. Look at your map and locate each of the following: Trenton, Princeton, Valley Forge, Lake Champlain, Lake Ontario, Oswego, Albany, Philadelphia, the Mohawk Valley, Ticonderoga, Bennington, and Saratoga.

3. Using a dictionary or an encyclopedia, make drawings of the American and British flags which were used during the Revolution.

4. Make a list of the important American generals.

Coming Up in Chapter 7

The Revolution becomes an international war . . . Victory at sea . . . The British surrender at Yorktown.

Questions for Your Classroom Discussions

1. Do you believe that the American victories at Saratoga marked "the turning point of the war"? Explain your answer.

2. Would you say that the American Revolution was a civil war? Why?

After the Americans had won at Saratoga, Ben Franklin, as America's Ambassador in Paris, got France to recognize American independence. Here, he is at the Court of King Louis XVI.

Chapter 7

The French Alliance

British General Burgoyne's defeat at Saratoga caused as much excitement in other countries as in Great Britain. Benjamin Franklin, America's ambassador in Paris, got France to recognize America's independence at once. The pro-American members of the British Parliament asked Lord North, the Prime Minister, to make peace.

The Prime Minister himself was afraid that France and America had signed a military treaty. British officials were sent to America with an offer to repeal the Intolerable Acts and cancel the war debts. The Continental Congress refused to settle for anything less than Britain's official recognition of America's independence; also, all British

Washington's men, wrapped in Dutch blankets, at the camp at Valley Forge huddled around fires, while the officers kept warm in military cloaks and great-coats which reached down almost to their ankles.

troops were to leave America at once. Lord North had waited too long.

France made an alliance with America and entered the war in February, 1778. Both countries agreed not to make peace with England without each other's consent. Both countries agreed to help each other in trade.

Even Spain and the Netherlands sided with America against England. Spain entered the war in 1779, with the understanding that she would get back Florida and Gibraltar. In 1780, Great Britain went to war with the Netherlands to stop her from trading with the United States.

To help the Americans, France brought troops and money. Most important, she brought her navy. Britain had to fight the French and Spanish navies so as to get back her control of the seas.

Before France's entry into the war, America had hardly any fighting ships. With Spain coming in on America's side, New Orleans, which belonged to Spain, soon became an important naval base. This added to England's problems at sea.

The British had to change their plans when the French took sides with the Americans. As a first step, they changed generals.

While General Washington was having such a hard time and

George Washington took time out during the winter at Valley Forge to pray on bended knee in the woods.

losing so many men in the extreme cold at Valley Forge, the British, in Philadelphia only twenty miles away, were living in comfort. By June, 1778, General Washington gathered together what was left of his forces and came out of his hiding place. The new British general, Henry Clinton, had been ordered to leave for New York, and General Washington pursued him

Because of the short supply of food and clothing, the men at Valley Forge often fought among themselves and even with their officers.

At the Battle of Monmouth, New Jersey, a woman named Molly Pitcher took her place with the men and fed the cannon.

across New Jersey. The armies collided at Monmouth, New Jersey, where they fought a lively battle. In the end, neither side won. (See map on page 53.)

British privateers were as damaging to America's ships as American privateers were to Britain's. Captain John Paul Jones, now commanding the *Bon Homme Richard*, an old ship given to America by the French government, took many prizes in English waters. In September, 1779, Jones had his greatest sea fight when he took on the *Serapis,* the pride of the British navy.

The *Serapis* had 54 guns, and Jones's ship had 42. During the three-hour battle, Jones tied the two ships together. The *Serapis* surrendered, but the *Bon Homme Richard* was so badly damaged that it sank two days later, after Jones had put his crew on the British ship. It was at the height of this battle that the British shouted, "Do you give up?" and Jones shouted back his never-to-be-forgotten line: "I have not yet begun to fight."

Meanwhile, in upper New York, the pro-British Indians were making trouble every day, until an American army burned the Iroquois villages in 1778. In that same year, a patriot frontiersman named George Rogers Clark made his way down the Ohio

John Paul Jones in the "Bon Homme Richard" (flying the American flag) came so close to the British ship, the "Serapis," that he was able to throw a rope across and tie the two ships together.

River and up the Mississippi, taking British forts along the way, including an important one at a town known as Vincennes. The hated British commander at Detroit, Colonel William Hamil-

The patriot frontiersman George Rogers Clark led his 120 men 180 miles through swamps and woods to retake Fort Vincennes.

Major John Andre, serving in the American army, turned out to be a British spy who was carrying messages to Benedict Arnold who was an American general. Arnold was planning to join the British when Andre was captured with secret papers and gave the story away.

ton, retook Vincennes, offering Indians rewards for American scalps. Clark then performed one of the most remarkable feats of the war. With some 120 men, he marched 180 miles to Vincennes —cold and hungry—and forced Hamilton to give up. By February, 1779, the entire western lands were free of British forces.

The French alliance of 1778 had brought new hope for only a short time to the war-weary Americans. Civilians and soldiers alike had no patience and little energy to push the war forward. The states paid little attention to the demands of Congress for more help. There were not enough supplies and troops. To make things worse, the French alliance had made the British fight harder.

The British were quick to take advantage of the great weariness of the patriots. Many Americans, tempted by easy money, became

Loyalists. General Benedict Arnold went over to the British side in the summer of 1779. His assignment was to gain West Point for the British. Arnold might have succeeded, if Major John Andre, a British spy sent to tell him what to do, had not been caught behind the American lines with his secret papers, and shot.

The last battles of the American Revolution were fought in the South. A series of British victories led General Clinton to believe that the British had permanently taken the Southern colonies. After the fall of Savannah at the end of 1778, the British had overrun all of Georgia. In May, 1780, General Benjamin Lincoln, leading American troops, had surrendered at Charleston with over 5,000 men.

And Lord Cornwallis, a first-rate British general, had defeated General Gates, the American commander, at Camden,

South Carolina, in August, 1780. So, the British held both Georgia and South Carolina. They might have done better but for Francis Marion, the "Swamp Fox,"

(Above) The Americans were fighting a losing battle around the harbor at Charleston, South Carolina.

(Below) Francis Marion got his name of the "Swamp Fox" by taking his troops into swamps and woods to fight the British.

The Marquis de Lafayette brought good news from Paris: France would be an ally of America and send soldiers and naval forces.

whose guerrilla warfare slowed them down.

The British, turning to North Carolina, were suddenly checked by defeats. At King's Mountain, near the state line, some 1,000 Loyalists were killed by backwoods patriots in October, 1780. Three months later, a heavy attack by the Continental Army at Guilford Courthouse forced Cornwallis to leave North Carolina and head for Yorktown, Virginia. General Nathanael Greene had replaced General Gates as commander of the Continental Army in the South. It was he who cleared the British out of most of South Carolina in 1781, and out of Charleston in late 1782.

Cornwallis had some 7,000 troops at Yorktown. With a string of powerful British ships standing by, he was certain that he and his men could easily escape by sea, if they had to. Of course, he had no way of knowing that a French fleet under Admiral de Grasse was, at that very moment, sailing north from the West Indies. He also did not know that the Frenchmen, led by General Rochambeau, would be on hand to support Washington, now on his way from New York.

The joint land-and-sea operation went off smoothly. De Grasse's ships, helped by others from Newport, Rhode Island, defeated the powerful British fleet on which Cornwallis was depending. At Yorktown, Washington's main army joined forces led by his friend, the Marquis de Lafayette, and by General Anthony Wayne. Cornwallis was now trapped between the French fleet and a French-American army of 16,000 men. He had no choice but to give up. As his

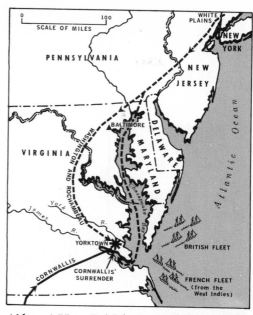

(Below) General Washington and the French general, Rochambeau, joined forces and ordered their combined armies to travel from White Plains, New York, to Yorktown, Virginia.

(Above) How British General Cornwallis was defeated on the peninsula near Yorktown, Virginia.

Painting by A. Couder from Museum at Versailles

Pleading illness, Cornwallis sent his second in command, Brigadier Charles O'Hara, to make the formal surrender of the British to General Benjamin Lincoln, whom Washington named to receive him.

defeated men dropped their arms, an American band played a sad tune called *The World Turned Upside Down.*

Lafayette announced the surrender to the French government. Serving under Lafayette had been a black American named James Armstead, who won his freedom by serving as a spy. A messenger carried the news of the surrender to the Continental Congress, now back in Philadelphia.

When Lord North in London heard of Cornwallis's defeat, he threw up his arms and cried, "O, God! it is all over." He was right—the war soon came to an end.

The peace treaty that followed raised a number of problems, which took time to solve. Talks began shortly after Cornwallis's surrender. But the final treaty, called the Treaty of Paris, was not finished for more than a year.

Benjamin Franklin, John Jay, John Adams, and Henry Laurens, the United States delegation, could hardly have gotten better terms: Great Britain recognized America's independence, making Canada the northern boundary, Florida the southern, and the Mississippi River the western. British troops were to leave the United States "with all convenient speed."

The Treaty of Paris contained no commercial agreement with

At the signing of the Peace Treaty of Paris in 1783 were the Americans John Jay, John Adams, Ben Franklin and Henry Laurens, along with Franklin's son, William Temple Franklin. They are shown left to right in this painting.

Unfinished painting by Benjamin West

Great Britain and left many questions unanswered. For one thing, the boundary lines were not clear. But America's independence was now certain. The large territory to the west, between the Appalachian Mountains and the Mississippi River, was now wide open for settlement.

The Americans actually came out of the war far better than their allies. Spain got Florida, but not Gibraltar. France got a few small islands and some trading posts in India and Senegal. But the war had left France with a debt as heavy as the British debt that had helped to bring about the war in the first place.

In war, nobody wins.

Things to Remember about Chapter 7

Meanings of Words and Phrases

Alliance: Any union or connection of interests between persons or nations.

Pro-American: One who likes America.

Pro-British: One who favors Great Britain and Britishers.

Officially recognize: When one country agrees that the new government of another country is going to last, and it sends an ambassador.

Treaty: An agreement between two or more nations in reference to peace, trade, or other international relations.

Scalp: The skin of the top of the head, including hair, which the Indians cut off their victims.

Feat: An act of great bravery or skill.

The signatures on the Treaty of Paris.

Meanings of Words and Phrases

Guerilla warfare: Fighting from bushes, forests and swamps, where the fighters cannot be easily seen.

Joint operation: Two people or groups working together.

Check Your Memory

1. What American victory brought about the American-French treaty? (See page 57.)

2. Where did the Americans and the French finally defeat the British? (See page 65.)

3. Where did the Treaty of Paris place the new boundaries of the United States? (See page 66.)

Projects

1. France contributed troops, money, and ships to the American cause. Arrange these in the order of their importance to the United States, and write a short report explaining your reasons.

Take a public opinion poll in your class on how they stand on the ideas you have arranged in the order of their importance. Make a bar graph showing how many are for, against, not sure.

2. Collect stamps and coins showing pictures of Washington, Lafayette, Franklin, and others who took part in the main events of the American Revolution.

3. Draw an outline map of the United States, and show in color the provisions of the Treaty of Paris of 1783.

Coming Up in Chapter 8

America moves ahead . . . The settlement of the western frontier . . . Shays' Rebellion.

Questions for Your Classroom Discussions

1. Look at your map and locate Yorktown, Virginia. If you were General Cornwallis would you station your men there? How would you have fought?

2. If you had been one of the representatives of the United States in 1783, would you have accepted all the terms of the Treaty of Paris? Describe the changes you might have made.

3. Why was the American Revolution an important event in world history?

Chapter 8

Postwar Problems and Development

America had many problems in 1783. One of the most serious was whether the 13 states, which had been united in war, would remain united in peace. As it turned out, the people under the new United States of America developed both a new spirit and a brand-new form of government in a very short time.

In 1775, even before the Revolution began, the colonial governments under the King were beginning to show signs of falling apart. Many of the royal governors and members of colonial legislatures had been frightened by the battles of Lexington, Concord, and Bunker Hill, and had returned to England. Only the local governments, now in the hands of patriots, continued to meet.

The Continental Congress had no power to act for any one of the colonies. Clearly, something had to be done to bring the colonies together under a single government. A year before the Declaration of Independence was written, the delegates to the Congress had adopted a resolution in 1775 to organize new governments to replace the old. John Adams called it "the most important resolution that was ever taken in America."

New Hampshire and South Carolina, both controlled by patriots, had already written new state constitutions. Within the next few months, all of the other states—except Connecticut, Rhode Island, and Massachusetts —did the same. Connecticut and Rhode Island had been self-governing colonies since their beginnings. Massachusetts, however, operated under a temporary government until close to the end of the Revolution.

Even though the colonists were fighting for the right to govern themselves, most of them

During the postwar period, Washington and his generals gathered in Fraunces Tavern on Broad Street, New York City. A black named Samuel Fraunces, who was the manager, is shown in the back near the doorway. Fraunces had been a former steward to George Washington.

had little or nothing to do with the writing of the new constitutions. In most states, the legislatures prepared the constitutions without questioning the settlers. Only in Massachusetts and New Hampshire did the people have a chance to accept or reject what their legislatures did.

Needless to say, the Declaration of Independence helped greatly to shape the new state constitutions. The first aim of the patriots who wrote them was to get iron-clad "guarantees" (promises) of man's "unalienable rights," among which were "life, liberty, and the pursuit of happiness."

As a direct result, each new state constitution began with a so-called "Bill of Rights," which promised: (1) religious freedom to worship or not; (2) the right to speak without censorship (free speech) and to publish anything (free press); (3) the right to gather; (4) the right to a fair trial by jury; and (5) equality of all citizens in the courts.

The patriots wanted the guarantees to be put into

"written constitutions," and to become the basic law of each state. Then, when someone had a question as to his rights under the law, all one had to do was to turn to the written law itself. The written law, not the opinion of some official, would give the answer. The new states were to be "governments of laws, and not of men."

The states also guaranteed the separation of church and state. What did this mean? The church was to have no part in government. At the start of the Revolution, the people of nine of the 13 colonies had to pay taxes for the support of an official state church. By 1787, however, there were official churches in only three of the states—New Hampshire, Massachusetts, and Connecticut. In all of the other states, the official churches had been closed down. The people were free to contribute to the church of their own choice, or pay nothing.

The fact of slavery troubled many Americans. Speaking out in 1773, Patrick Henry said: "No man has the right to keep another in chains. Let us not forget that all men are born free and equal." A number of slaveowners who agreed with Henry freed their slaves. Many states passed laws that would soon provide for the freeing of slaves and the abolition, or the ending, of slavery. Quork Walker, a Massachusetts slave,

won his freedom using Patrick Henry's argument.

By 1776, it had become quite clear that the 13 states had to be really united. But in what kind of union? And what sort of government should they create?

Ben Franklin and a number of other delegates to the Continental Congress wanted to build a strong central government. Franklin listened to the objections. One delegate said, "The states were fighting a war to win their independence . . . Why, then, should they create an American government that might turn out to be as tyrannical as the British government had been?"

Franklin came up with this answer: "Without a union we shall not be able to win our independence; without a union we shall not be able to become a nation."

The Congress loudly applauded Franklin. A committee was named to prepare a plan of union. A week after Independence Day, July 4, the committee, headed by John Dickinson of Pennsylvania, presented a long document entitled the "Articles of Confederation." Over a year was to pass, however, before the delegates to the Congress could all agree with what the committee had prepared. Finally, in November, 1777, the Congress voted to adopt the plan.

The Articles of Confederation established a confederation, or league, of free and independent states known as "The United States of America." The central government of the league was to consist of a Congress having from two to seven delegates from each state. Each state was to have only one vote in the Congress. The Congress could pass a law whenever nine states, large or small, voted for it. No change could be made in the Articles without all of the states voting for it.

But this was only the first step in the creation of the United States. Before the Articles could be made to work, each of the 13 states had to ratify, or approve, the plan. It was not until 1781 that all of the states agreed to enter the Confederation. Maryland was the last to come in.

The main reason for the delay was "land-grabbing." About half of the states claimed lands between the Appalachian Mountains and the Mississippi River. Many of the claims overlapped, particularly in the Old Northwest—the land north of the Ohio River. When two or more states claimed the same territory, there was no way of deciding which state really owned the land.

The states without claims to the western lands caused the worst problems. Maryland, for example, refused to join the Confederation until all of the states gave up their claims.

The Articles were an attempt to provide a written plan for the new nation. The attempt, as we shall see, was successful in some ways and unsuccessful in others.

In gaining control of the vast Northwest Territory, the Confederation became, in effect, a "colonial power." So America now had to face the same sort of problems that Great Britain had to face when she set up colonies in the New World.

There were many questions. How was the land to be distributed among the men and women who "colonized" this new frontier? Who was to profit from the sale of land— the land speculators or the settlers? Who was to make the laws for the towns—the government or the settlers? The future of the United States depended to a large extent upon the answers.

In the next few years, Congress moved from place to place. It went first to Princeton, New Jersey, in June, 1783; then to Annapolis, Maryland, in November; to Trenton, New Jersey, in 1784; and a year later to New York City, where it stayed until the Confederation ended. Yet, during this time, Congress passed a series of ordinances, or laws, which set the pattern of government land policies for over 100 years.

The Land Ordinance of 1785 allowed the government to

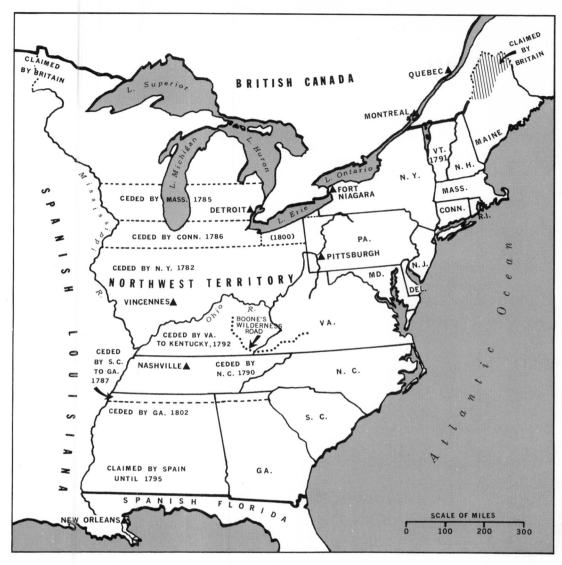

How the states gave up their lands in the Northwest Territory.

survey, or measure off, the Northwest Territory into "townships," each 6 miles square. Each township was to be divided into 36 smaller squares of 640 acres, or one square mile, to be known as "sections." One section in every township was to be sold or rented to provide money for public schools. Four other sections were to be set aside for the United States Government. The remaining 31 sections were to be sold by the government at a price of not less than one dollar an acre. This Ordinance offered many advantages for the development of the West. Settlements, close together, would be safer from Indian attacks. Even more important, the sale of land would give the government the money it needed to meet its expenses and pay part of the war debt.

The Northwest Ordinance of 1787 provided for the governing of the Northwest Territory. It was to be ruled by a governor and three judges named by Congress. When the population reached a total of 5,000 free males of voting age, the settlers might elect a legislature to pass laws for themselves. They might also name a delegate to speak for them, but not to vote in Congress. When the population of any part of the territory reached a total of 60,000, the people could draw up a constitution. Once this constitution had been approved by Congress, that part of the Territory could become a state. Not less than three nor more than five states were to be carved out of the Northwest Territory. A new state

would have the same powers and rights as any one of the 13 original states. Public schools were to be established. Slavery would *not* be allowed.

The advantages to new settlers were quite clear. They could own large lots of cheap land, they would have free schools, they would be free to go to the church of their choice, the area would become a state as it grew, and no one would be a slave.

Among the pioneers who braved the wilderness and led settlers into the huge Northwest Territory was a man named Daniel Boone. In 1775, before the Revolution, he opened up a path to Kentucky called the Wilderness Trail. By 1792, the population of the territory had reached 60,000. Kentucky then adopted a constitution and became a state. The Wilderness Trail, lengthened to 300 miles by Boone, became one of the main roads to the frontier.

There were "makings of

74

Washington resigning his commission as Commander-in-Chief of the American armies at the State House in Annapolis, Maryland.

revolt," as George Washington said, in almost every state in 1786-87. But only in Massachusetts did a revolt break out. Before the Revolution, the earnings of Massachusetts farmers had come largely from the sale

Daniel Boone, famous frontiersman from Kentucky, shows his black helper where he wants to be buried.

of farm products to the British West Indies. After the break with Great Britain, this market was closed to them. Massachusetts farmers found it more and more difficult to pay their taxes and the debts on their farms. Many of them were so poor they were almost forced to live on bread and water. To make things worse, businessmen, mostly from Boston, controlled the state legislature. These men managed to pass new laws that shifted more taxes onto the farmers. Among these was a heavy tax on land.

During the summer of 1786, farmers held town meetings, demanding relief from the taxes. But the Massachusetts legislature refused to act. Farm after farm was seized for non-payment of taxes and debts.

Many of the farmers took matters into their own hands. One group led by Daniel Shays, who had been a captain in the Continental Army, tried to

Daniel Shays started the rebellion named for him with the aim of capturing guns at the Springfield, Massachusetts, arsenal.

capture the arsenal at Springfield in an attempt to get guns. But the men were too poorly armed to succeed.

Frightened by this attempt, a number of Bostonians raised money to equip a militia to put down what they chose to call "Shays' Rebellion." The troops, chasing Shays and his men through the woods, killed many and drove others into Vermont.

Except for a few small fights in other parts of Massachusetts, the revolt was crushed. Luckily, Massachusetts pardoned fourteen of the leaders, including Shays, or let them off with short prison terms. A newly elected legislature granted the farmers most of their demands. In 1787, business improved and more people got jobs.

Things to Remember about Chapter 8

Meanings of Words and Phrases

Postwar: After the fighting ended.

Legislature: A law-making body.

Temporary: For the time being, not permanent.

Constitution: The system of principles and laws under which a government is organized.

Guarantee: A promise to do something.

Abolition: Ending.

Union: Any joining together.

Meanings of Words and Phrases

Confederation: A type of union. A league of independent states.

Ratify: To approve.

Land-grabbing: Taking land illegally.

Land speculator: A person who buys and sells land with the hope of making a profit.

Ordinance: Any law made by a government.

Survey: To measure or study something, such as land.

Arsenal: An armory where guns are made or stored; a collection of weapons.

Check Your Memory

1. What five important rights did the Bill of Rights guarantee? (See page 70.)

2. In what ways did the Articles of Confederation establish a central government? (See pages 71-72.)

3. What advantages were provided by the Land Ordinance of 1785 and the Northwest Ordinance of 1787? (See pages 72-74.)

Projects

1. Locate on a map all the places where Congress met from the time of its first meeting as the Continental Congress.

2. Since the end of World War II in 1945, a number of foreign colonies in Africa, Asia and the Near East, inspired by the American example, have won their independence. Look up and list as many of these new nations as you can.

3. Compare the United Nations attempts to solve problems of small and large nations with the problems of new states and territories faced by the Second Continental Congress.

4. Study the Northwest Ordinance of 1787. Join in a classroom campaign to help people understand the attractions of moving West. Make a poster with catchy slogans to advertise the good points of the Ordinance.

Coming Up in Chapter 9

The Founding Fathers . . . The American Constitution . . . George Washington, the first President.

Questions for Your Classroom Discussions

1. What would have happened if there had not been separation of church and state in the United States?

2. If you had been a farmer in Massachusetts in 1786-87, would you have taken part in Shays' Rebellion? Give reasons for your answer.

3. Why did this rebellion alarm American leaders?

Chapter 9

A New Kind of Government

Many of General Washington's friends wanted him to run the United States by himself. The General was against the idea. He wanted America to be a "democracy," not a "monarchy." He knew, too, that a King George I of America would be opposed as much as a King George III of England.

The new nation, as we know, was faced with many problems. The federal government was too weak. The Congress could make laws, but there was no department or official to see that they were carried out. America owed money to the private bankers and other citizens who had helped win the Revolution. Also, she owed money to France and the Netherlands. The Congress, without money, could not pay these loans.

Under the Articles of Confederation, the states were supposed to give money to the government. But when the Congress asked for dollars, they did nothing about it. The government had no power to collect taxes directly from the people.

General Washington took leave of his officers and soon afterwards was offered the "throne" as King of America but he refused. He wanted America to be a "democracy."

Still another weakness of the government was its lack of power to control trade. This caused trouble not only inside but outside the United States. Each state had the right to tax goods brought in from foreign countries. Each state placed its own special taxes on goods of foreign merchants who traded with America. To European nations it seemed that each state was itself an independent country.

Besides this, each state had the right to tax goods brought in from other states. New York, for example, could tax fish brought in from Massachusetts. These taxes kept people from buying and selling freely to each other. The states got into many arguments. None of them got settled, because the United States had neither a court nor a judge to decide such arguments.

It is no wonder that foreign nations had little respect for America's weak government. Some countries seemed to question if America was really a nation. When the Congress sent John Adams of Massachusetts to England as America's ambassador, one British official jokingly asked him where the other 12 state representatives were.

In 1787, there were some four million Americans living in the United States. Most of them spoke English. But even the same language could not hold together a people so widely scattered.

Almost all of them lived east of the Appalachian Mountains, between Maine and Florida. Others had gone on to settle in what are now Kentucky and Tennessee, where they were almost completely cut off from the people living along the Atlantic Coast.

There was no fast or easy way to travel. People rode on horses, in stagecoaches or in wagons. There was no fast or easy way to communicate. Newspapers reported local news mainly. The people of one state knew little or nothing about the people of another. James Madison of Virginia, a well-educated man, once said: "I know as much about what is happening in the Carolinas as I know about what is happening in Europe." He meant he knew little about either.

Some patriots, like Washington, were deeply worried over the weaknesses of the Articles of Confederation. What they wanted was a constitution that would provide a whole new plan of government, including laws for governing the nation. The Constitutional Convention, which met in Philadelphia from May 25 to September 17, 1789, did just that—it took on the job of drawing up this constitution.

Of the 55 delegates, representing 12 of the 13 states, two were college presidents; three were teachers or had been; 26 others were college graduates;

James Madison, although he was only in his 30's at the time, was one of the "Founding Fathers" and the "architect" of the Constitution.

four had studied law; nine were foreign born; one was a farmer; 28 had served in the Continental Congress; and most of the others had been members of state legislatures. Rhode Island did not approve of the Convention, and sent nobody.

Perhaps the most surprising thing about the delegates, who were called the "Founding Fathers," was their youth. Nine of them, including James Madison, were between 30 and 35. Not all were young. George Washington, who was suffering from arthritis and who would have been much happier at home, was 55. Only four delegates had passed the age of 60. Benjamin Franklin, at 81, was the eldest statesman by 15 years.

John Adams and Thomas Jefferson, in Europe on government business, did not get to the Convention. Washington was named president of the group. Armed guards stood at the doors to meeting rooms to give the delegates full secrecy and freedom to talk. No one but the delegates knew what progress was being made.

Thomas Jefferson had said in the Declaration of Independence that the chief rights of men were "life, liberty, and the pursuit of happiness." But property (land and possessions) was clearly the most important thing in the minds of the Founding Fathers.

To most of these men of property, the words "life" and "liberty" meant freedom for other Americans to try and become rich and powerful, too. Madison looked at it this way: it was not their idea to give away their property to try to make all men equal. "Equality would drag down the good rather than raise the bad," he said.

True, the Constitution of the United States was written by men of property. But it was also written to make one strong, united nation out of 13 very different states. The Constitutional Convention agreed to a plan that called for a Congress of two houses—a Senate and a House of Representatives, which together would form the "legislative branch" of the government. In

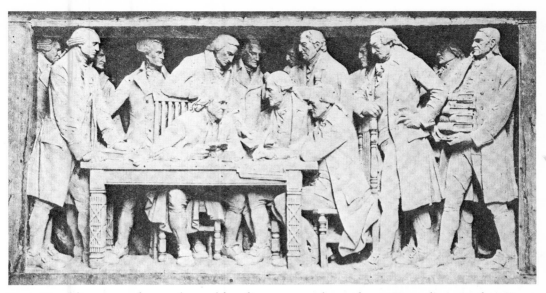

Ben Franklin, seated at the table, listens to the other "Founding Fathers" as the Constitution is prepared. This model is for a stone sculpture in the Nebraska State Capitol building in Lincoln, Nebraska.

the Senate, each state would have two Senators, each serving six years at a time. To the House of Representatives, each state would send one Representative for every 30,000 people, each serving two years at a time. Each state would have the same number of votes (two) in the Senate. In the House of Representatives, a state would have as many votes as its population entitled it to have. Thus, the make-up of the Senate would please the small states. And the make-up of the House of Representatives would please the large states.

To please the South, the Convention delegates agreed to count a slave as "three-fifths of a free man" as a base for electing Representatives and paying taxes. In addition, they agreed to place no taxes on exports and no restrictions on the importing of slaves for 20 years.

All foreign treaties would have to be approved by two-thirds of the Senate. To please the North, they agreed that a majority vote of Congress would be enough to pass any laws controlling trade.

The "executive branch" of the government was to be put in the hands of a President, to be chosen every four years by a so-called "Electoral College," itself picked by the legislatures or the people of the states. The President would have the right to enforce laws, make treaties, command the army and navy, and appoint judges. He also could name a Cabinet to advise him, consisting of a Secretary of State, Secretary

George Washington addressing the delegates to the Constitutional Convention, held at Independence Hall, Philadelphia.

of the Treasury, and Secretary of War.

A Supreme Court, made up of nine Justices appointed by the President, would also be created to interpret and explain the Constitution and federal law. This was to be known as the "judicial branch" of the government.

The value of the dollar was to be protected by forbidding the states to pay their debts in anything but silver or gold. The states were to be protected by keeping those rights which were not given to the federal government.

The Constitution was short, but it allowed room for improvement. Even though it was built, in the words of James Madison, "for the ages," it could be amended, or added to and changed. A Bill of Rights consisting of 10 "amendments" or additions was, indeed, promised to prevent the federal government from attacking personal rights.

The Constitution caused many exciting discussions and debates in the Constitutional Convention. It was not accepted easily by the states, either. (North Carolina and Rhode Island did not become states until 1789 and 1790.) The Constitution had not been written, as Washington himself demanded, simply to "please the people." Alexander Hamilton of New York considered it "frail (weak) and worthless." John Dickinson of Delaware, a believer in democracy, was against any idea of "weaving into the Constitution a respect for wealth." Benjamin Franklin, a friend of the poor, expressed his dislike of anything that worked to "lower the common people."

The Constitution was finally accepted or "ratified" in June, 1788. It promised a better government than the Articles of Confederation. Each state or selfish group in the states felt that it could influence or delay some branch of government. As Madison complained during the Convention, "There was too much thought about the need of opposing" instead of uniting and being fair.

In any event, a system of "checks and balances" was written into the Constitution. This allowed each branch of government the power to keep another branch from going beyond its powers. For example, only the "legislative branch" could give money for the "executive branch" to use; the "judicial branch" would decide if a law passed by the "legislative branch" were in keeping with the Constitution.

Under the Constitution, no one could take away a person's liberty—if he were free to start with. The Constitution even provided for its own change.

Everyone knew that George Washington would be elected the first President of the United

Federal Hall in New York City stands on the spot at Nassau and Wall Streets where George Washington took the oath of office as first President of the United States in 1789.

States. No man was more capable, more loved, or more respected. On April 30, 1789, he walked out onto the balcony of Federal Hall, New York City, then the national capital, to say: "I do solemnly swear that I will faithfully execute the office of President of the United States and will, to the best of my ability, preserve, protect, and defend the Constitution of the United States." This is the same oath of office used today.

John Adams, who was elected Vice President, said that he was "afraid that the Republic would not last beyond his lifetime."

Things to Remember about Chapter 9

Meanings of Words and Phrases

Monarchy: A country ruled by a king or queen.

Federal: Refers to the "national government" as opposed to the separate state governments.

Ambassador: A person appointed to travel to another capital to represent his country.

Appalachians: A chain of mountains going north and south, inland from the Atlantic coast of the United States.

Convention: A large meeting of delegates.

Majority vote: More than one half of the total vote.

Cabinet: The men who advise the President of the United States, such as the Secretary of State, Secretary of the Treasury and others in the "executive branch" of government.

Interpret: Explain the law or any statement.

Debate: A discussion by two or more people with differing views.

Amend: To add to or change.

Checks and balances: A system by which each branch of government (legislative, executive and judicial) has certain powers that are not greater than the powers of the other branches.

Republic: A nation in which most of the people can vote.

Check Your Memory

1. What were the chief weaknesses of the Articles of Confederation? (See pages 78-79.)

2. In what ways did the Constitution please the demands of the large and small states? (See pages 80-81.)

3. What did the Constitutional Convention do to please the South in respect to slavery and trade? (See page 81.)

The first presidential mansion was at Pearl and Cherry Streets in New York City, the first capital of the United States.

Check Your Memory

4. What important advantage did the system of "checks and balances" provide? (See page 83.)

5. What words were used by Presidents Dwight D. Eisenhower, John F. Kennedy, Lyndon B. Johnson and Richard M. Nixon when they were sworn in as President? (See page 84.)

Projects

1. Imagine that you were a member of the Constitutional Convention. Prepare (a) a short speech that you might make in support of ratification; (b) a short speech against ratification.

2. With your teacher, read the original document of the Constitution of the United States and discuss it.

3. Make a "family tree" of the government as it was organized under the Constitution.

Coming Up in Chapter 10

The Whisky Rebellion . . . George Washington retires . . . The Federalists and anti-Federalists.

Questions for Your Classroom Discussions

1. If you had been living in 1788, what arguments would you have given to support the new Constitution?

2. In what ways did the new Constitution correct the weaknesses of the Articles of Confederation?

Overlooking the Potomac River is Mt. Vernon, the home of George Washington from 1747 until his death in 1799.

Chapter 10

The Young Republic

President Washington had to start "from scratch" (from the very beginning) when he set up the new government in 1789. He had been left nothing by the Confederation, except a few clerks, an empty treasury, and a heavy debt. The navy, built by the Continental Congress, no longer existed. The army, by this time, had but 700 officers and men. There were, as yet, no federal laws, no courts, no law-enforcement officers, and no method for collecting taxes.

Luckily, there were a few

things to the good. By 1790, when the capital was moved from New York City to Philadelphia, a time of good trade had returned. Virginia and the Carolinas had gotten back most of their prewar foreign trade. The farmers in Europe had had a bad year and this had built up demand for wheat grown by farmers of the Middle States. New England's West Indian trade had returned to normal. Important new markets had been opened by American ships traveling to China, India, and Russia.

Washington thought in terms of the whole nation rather than about his own state of Virginia, or any other state. He was President of *all* the people. His army life had given him a wide knowledge of men from all parts of America. Also, he was able to get along with all kinds of people. He had learned how to bring out the good qualities of able men while overlooking their bad qualities.

For the heads of three government departments—State, Treasury, and War—Washington had few men to pick from. The American Confederation had offered little chance for leadership.

For Secretary of State, an important office in the President's Cabinet, a diplomat was needed. Franklin, best trained for the job, was too old. John Jay, a lawyer who had been a minister to Spain, was a possible choice, but he was passed by. A treaty he had made with Spain had proved to be unpopular. So Washington's choice was Thomas Jefferson, who had done well as Ambassador to France.

Robert Morris, a capable banker, refused the job of

From the engraving by H. S. Sadd after the painting by Tompkins H. Matteson

President Washington made his First Inaugural Address in the Senate chamber of Federal Hall, New York City.

Tom Jefferson was chosen by Washington as his Secretary of State.

Secretary of the Treasury. But he suggested Alexander Hamilton, who believed in a strong federal government, and this fitted in nicely with Washington's plans.

General Henry Knox continued as Secretary of War, as he had been for the American Confederation. Edmund Randolph, who had just finished his term as governor of Virginia, was appointed Attorney General to help the President on matters of law.

Samuel Osgood was named Postmaster General. Post Office business was to be managed by the Treasury Department.

Hamilton was quick to see and make use of two ways of solving the government's money problems. One was by placing tariffs, or customs duties, on imports, and by placing taxes on the manufacture, sale, or use of goods within the country. Just as important was his founding of the Bank of the United States, a national bank owned by both the government and private citizens. Whatever profits the bank made were to be divided between the government and the private citizens. The bank set up branches in many cities.

One of Hamilton's taxes led to trouble. In western Pennsylvania and in the Southern states, farmers were far from markets. Muddy roads made it hard for them to carry their grain (their wheat, corn and rye) to faraway towns near the Atlantic coast. Badly in need of money, many farmers took to using their grain for the making of whisky. Jugs of whisky could be moved easily and cheaply. Profits on whisky were good. To these farmers, Hamilton's tax on whisky seemed as unjust and tyrannical as the British Stamp Act had been to all Americans in 1765.

Pennsylvanians rebelled against Congress and refused to pay the tax. The federal government decided to show how strong it was. The Whisky Rebellion, as the movement was called, broke out in 1794. But it melted away when 15,000 troops were sent to the scene by President Washington. The ringleaders, caught and tried for treason, were pardoned by the President. It was a serious but successful test of the power of the federal government.

Hamilton's money-raising program was, on the whole, a success. The new government paid its bills honestly and quickly. The Bank of the United States issued money that everyone accepted. The import tax and other taxes brought in much-needed dollars.

To be sure, Hamilton's ideas put money into the pockets of the rich who bought shares in the Bank of the United States.

But they also helped *all* Americans by giving the United States a good money system and a good reputation that few of the older European nations enjoyed.

Jefferson kept the United States out of foreign wars. France had overthrown her king and started a republic, which copied many American ideas. Some European governments wanted at that time to crush France. It was Jefferson who warned against America's becoming an ally of *any* fighting nation. Greatly influenced by Jefferson, Washington stated his

George Washington and his family posed for this famous painting by Edward Savage, which now hangs in the National Gallery of Art, Washington, D.C.

The first Bank of the United States in Philadelphia was owned partly by the government and partly by citizens.

foreign policy in one word—peace. The President's Proclamation of Neutrality of 1793 stopped Americans from taking part in any fighting on land or at sea with any nation at war.

When George Washington insisted on leaving the Presidency in 1797, at the end of eight years, the people wanted him to stay on, but he refused. This started the custom of two terms for a President. Washington had every reason to feel pleased and said so in his "Farewell Address." The Constitution had been made to work. Three more states—Vermont, Kentucky and Tennessee—had joined the Union. The United States was accepted as a strong power. In spite of

attacks on American ships by the British and French, the United States was still at peace.

Even though he did not talk about it, Washington could also be proud of the first 10 amendments to the Constitution, which had been passed as promised. The first thing that Washington's government had done was to write the Bill of Rights, which guaranteed every American a number of liberties, including:

1. The right to worship as he pleased.

2. The right to assemble in peaceful meetings.

3. The right to say what he wanted in conversations, speeches, or in print.

4. The right to know the

charges brought against him if arrested, and to receive a prompt trial.

5. The right to a trial by a jury of ordinary citizens, if accused of a crime.

6. The right to force the government to pay him a fair price for any property of his that the government might take for public use.

The Bill of Rights, ratified by the states in 1791, has remained as one of the main features of the Constitution. No document in American history, except perhaps the Declaration of Independence, has been admired more deeply by the people.

Yet Washington felt unhappy about what proved to be the most lasting thing of his Administration—the beginning of political parties.

Jefferson and Hamilton, both close to Washington, agreed with the President's ideas, but disagreed as to the ways of carrying them out.

Hamilton and his friends sided with England in her fight with France and opposed the French Revolution. They even tried to push President Washington into going to war on the side of the British. Hamilton and his party, called Federalists, wanted a strong central government, or Federalism.

Against them stood Jefferson and the Republicans, or anti-Federalists, who agreed with and supported the French Revolution. They stood for the farmers and States' Rights against federal power.

In short, here is how the two patriots stood: Hamilton wanted to keep the government's power in one central place. Jefferson wanted to spread it around. Hamilton feared trouble would result from too little government. Jefferson feared tyranny would result from too much government. Hamilton wanted to improve American ways of doing business by encouraging manufacturing and shipping. Jefferson wanted to keep America a nation of farmers. Hamilton, who

Tony Washington, who entertained President Washington with his fiddle playing, was one of many slaves who took their owner's last name.

had never left America, wanted to make it like Europe. Jefferson, who knew Europe, wanted to make America as unlike Europe as possible.

Hamilton and Jefferson were as opposite as two men could be. Jefferson left the Cabinet in 1793, Hamilton in 1794, but Washington remained friends with both.

Meanwhile, a problem had risen among the settlers in the Northwest Territory. They felt that the government did not protect them enough against Indian attacks. The British and the Spanish had stirred up the Indians, trying to keep Americans from moving westward. The settlers also felt that the Federalists had been interested only in trade, industry, and good relations with England.

The settlers were especially unhappy about the Jay Treaty, signed in London in 1794. This treaty, by making the British give up forts in the Northwest Territory, may have prevented a

When George Washington died in 1799, Alexander Hamilton said: "He was like a father . . . and very necessary to me." Washington was also the "father of his country."

war. But it recognized British claims in some parts of the Northwest Territory already settled by Americans.

Making the most of this unrest, Jefferson and Madison formed a Committee of Correspondence with two purposes: to spread anti-Federalist stories and to prevent New England industry from growing. Besides this, they organized a new Republican political group in New York City, called the Tammany Society. Aaron Burr, at its head, was a clever politician and hated Hamilton.

However, the Federalist party held onto the Presidency in the election of 1796. Their candidate, John Adams, just beat Jefferson, who became Vice President.

The first banking house in Boston was this National Bank organized in 1784.

Meanings of Words and Phrases

Prewar: Before the war.

National: Concerning the nation as a whole.

Diplomat: A person employed by the State Department to conduct his country's business with another country.

Appoint: To choose.

Tariff: A customs duty, a tax on imports and exports.

Reputation: The standing of a nation in the eyes of the world.

Policy: A course of action followed by a government, business, or person.

Retire: To leave office and not run again.

Administration: Refers to the President and those who serve with him while he is in office.

Federalism: A system of government in which a written constitution divides governing powers between the federal government and the state governments. Both get their powers from a common document—the constitution—not from each other.

Federalist: One who believes in Federalism.

Anti-Federalist: One who is against Federalism.

States' Rights: The powers held by the states.

Check Your Memory

1. What were the most difficult problems faced by Washington in 1789? (See page 86.)

2. Who were the members of Washington's Cabinet? (See pages 87-88.)

3. What steps did Hamilton take to solve the nation's money problems? (See pages 88-89.)

4. What did Washington do to keep America out of war? (See page 90.)

Projects

1. Look at your map and locate the following places: Mount Vernon, New York City, Philadelphia, Pittsburgh, and western Pennsylvania. Start making a collection of picture postcards showing cities important to the early history of the United States.

2. Draw a cartoon on the Whisky Rebellion and the ways

it tested the strength of the new government.

3. Interpret the Bill of Rights in your own words to a second-grade class. Use a tape recorder, in school, to prepare your talk to hear how it sounds.

Coming Up In "A Fresh Look at American History," Volume 3

The Louisiana Purchase . . . Another war with Great Britain . . . The Monroe Doctrine . . . The growth of America . . . Slavery.

Questions for Your Classroom Discussions
1. From your point of view, how was the new government "undemocratic"?
2. In what ways did Jefferson and Hamilton differ from each other?
3. Would you have been a supporter of Jefferson or Hamilton? Why?

Index

Adams, John, 9, 30, 78, 84, 92
Adams, Samuel, 5, 7, 8–9, 22
Allen, Ethan, 23
Allen, Richard, 37
Arnold, Benedict, 27, 41, 54, 55, 62
Articles of Confederation, 71–72, 78
Attorney General, 88
Attucks, Crispus, 4, 9, 42
Bank of the United States, 88–89
Bill of Rights, 82, 90–91
blacks, in postwar period, 70
blacks, in Revolution, 4, 9, 20, 22, 26, 35,
    37, 42–43, 51
Boone, Daniel, 74, 75
Boston Massacre, 4, 9–10
Boston Port Act, 13
Boston Tea Party, 10
branches of government, 80–82
Brandywine, battle of, 52, 53
Breed's Hill, battle of, 24–26
British East India Company, 10, 13
Bunker Hill, battle of, 24–26
Burgoyne, General John, 51–55
Burke, Edmund, 17, 26
Burr, Aaron, 91
Cabinet, 81–82, 87–88
capitals of United States, 87
"checks and balances," 83
Clark, George Rogers, 60–62
Common Sense, 29–30
communications, 79
Concord, battle of, 21, 22–23, 24
Congress, 80–81
Congress, First Continental, 14–15
Congress, Provincial, 15
Congress, Second Continental, 24, 57
Constitution, 80–84
Constitutional Convention, 79–84
constitutions, written, 71
Continental Association, 15
Cornwallis, General, 62–66
Cuffe, Paul, 43

Declaration of Independence, 3, 29–37
Declaration of Rights, 15
Delaware River, crossing of, 51
Electoral College, 81
executive branch, 81–82
Federalists, 91
First Continental Congress, 14–15
flag, American, 50–51
"Founding Fathers," 80, 81
Franklin, Benjamin, 30, 31, 53, 57, 66,
    67, 71, 80, 81
Fraunces, Samuel, 70
French-American alliance, 58–67
Germantown, battle of, 53
Green Mountain Boys, 23, 54
Hale, Nathan, 48, 49
Hamilton, Alexander, 88–92
Hancock, John, 15–16, 22, 33
Henry, Patrick, 6–7, 14, 17, 19, 70
Herkimer, General Nicholas, 54
Hessian soldiers, 26, 32, 51, 54
House of Representatives, 80–81
Independence Hall, 34
Intolerable Acts, 13–14, 57
Jay, John, 67, 87
Jay Treaty, 91
Jefferson, Thomas, 3, 30, 31–32, 87,
    89–92
Jews in Revolution, 40, 41
Jones, John Paul, 45–46, 60
judicial branch, 82
Kosciusko, Thaddeus, 41
Lafayette, Marquis de, 65–66
Land Ordinance of 1785, 72–74
land policies, 72–76
Lee, Light-Horse Harry, 30
legislative branch, 80
Lexington, battle of, 20, 21–22, 24
Long Island, battle of, 47–48
Loyalists, 35, 36
Madison, James, 79, 80, 92
Marion, Francis, 63

"midnight ride," 21–22
minutemen, 16
Monmouth, battle of, 60
Mount Vernon, 86
navies, American, 44
Neutrality, Proclamation of, 90
non-importation agreement, 6, 29
Northwest Ordinance, 74
Northwest Territory, 72–74, 92
oath of office, Presidential, 84
Otis, James, 7
Paine, Thomas, 29, 30
parties, political, 91–92
Pitcher, Molly, 60
Poor, Salem, 20, 22
Postmaster General, 88
Presidential oath of office, 84
Princeton, battle of, 51
Proclamation of Neutrality, 90
Provincial Congress, 15
Pulaski, Count Casimir, 41
Quartering Act, 6
Quebec Act, 13
Republicans, 91
Revere, Paul, 21–22
Revolution, 21–68
"Revolutionary Tea" song, 12
Ross, Betsy, 51
Salem, Peter, 26
Salomon, Haym, 40, 41
Saratoga, battle of, 55
Second Continental Congress, 24, 57

Secretary of State, 87
Secretary of Treasury, 87, 88
Secretary of War, 87, 88
Senate, 80–81
Shays, Daniel, 75–76
Shays' Rebellion, 76
slavery, 71, 74, 81, 91
Sons of Liberty, 7
Spanish-American alliance, 58
Stamp Act of 1765, 6–8
state constitutions, 69–71
states' rights, 91, 93
Steuben, Baron Friedrich von, 41
Sugar Act of 1764, 5
"Swamp Fox," 63
Tammany Society, 91
Taxation, 6–10, 75–76, 78–79, 88–89
Ticonderoga, battle of, 23, 54
Townshend Acts, 8–9
Treaty of Paris, 66–67, 68
Trenton, battle of, 51
Valley Forge, 53, 58, 59
Vincennes, battle of, 61–62
Virginia Resolutions, 6
Washington, George, 9, 24, 39–46, 58–59,
    70, 74, 75, 78–79, 83, 86–94
Washington, Tony, 91
Wheatley, Phillis, 35
Whigs, 33
Whisky Rebellion, 88
"written constitutions," 71
Yorktown, battle of, 64–66